# Praise for *The Perfect Teacher Coach*

This is a book that will have a real impact on the development of coaching within schools. The authors present a straightforward yet powerful way of exploring and understanding the key aspects of building high quality coaching throughout a school.

Its simple, jargon free approach captures the concepts and practical elements that will help any school move towards a successful coaching culture.

Written from a 'reflective and emotionally intelligent mindset', the style of the book is utterly congruent with a coaching approach – encouraging the reader to question and challenge their own behaviours and thinking and become even better. Throughout, the passion and belief are evident and yet clear links to Ofsted and performance management frameworks ground it in the reality of today's schools.

Any school leader seeking to build sustainable progress in pupil learning at the same time as developing well-being and resilience in their staff will have a better journey with this book at their side.

Andy Vass, Professional Coach

*The Perfect Teacher Coach* is just like the authors: solution focused and easy to follow. It's a book you can read from cover to cover and know what you want to do next. But it's also a good book to dip into if you've done coaching before, to give you new techniques to try, and sometimes it's also good to have reassurance that what you're doing is right! In the absence of having one of the authors at the end of the phone, this book is the next best thing!

Charlotte Johnson, Vice Principal (teaching and learning)
Thomas Clarkson Academy Wisbech, Cambs

In good schools learning is fun, exciting, active, creative and developmental for teachers and for children. We all learn by mirroring ways of doing things from others who are excited by learning, positive, non-judgemental, keen to share and above all to listen.

Learning needs to take place in a secure environment where we have permission to take risks, experiment and at times make mistakes. Under these conditions all our learning journeys could be greatly enhanced by what I have described as a 'lead learner', someone brought into sharp focus in Jackie Beere and Terri Broughton's book – *The Perfect Teacher Coach*.

In my school this approach was developed through colleagues training in counselling at the Tavistock Clinic, taking part in the in-house Masters programme delivered for us by the Institute of Education, experiencing our many home-delivered inset sessions such as teachers becoming students for the day, following students, teaching other teachers or planning, discussing and team teaching together on a regular basis, as well as engaging in the many cross curricular events that took place. The staff rooms became hives of learning conversations and the school a learning community as well as a community of learners.

What this book does superbly is provide an aide memoire for leaders at all levels in schools (both teaching and associate staff too, colleagues who are supporting staff development, middle managers and all teams such as departments, years/houses as well as senior leadership) in how to conduct constructive learning conversations. It will also be of value for students training to be peer tutors or mentors.

The value of this approach is well documented in this book and will certainly lead to successful learning for all. It is the means of keeping a school climbing ever upwards, one of the greatest challenges for all schools, especially those that think they have arrived. You never arrive! But that is was makes the whole learning game so exiting, creative and rewarding. This book provides a crucial tool for raising the achievement of staff and students in all schools.

Dame Tamsyn Imison, Former Head Teacher, Hampstead School 1984-2000, Editor *Comprehensive Successes* and *All our geese are swans*, Institute of Education

*The Perfect Teacher Coach* has a very friendly and easy to navigate layout, which allows you to follow the book and take a step-by-step approach to techniques and theories or 'dip into' and refresh skills that you haven't used for a while.

Jackie and Terri are clearly passionate about the difference that coaching can make in an educational setting and this comes across loud and clear. The references to Ofsted and CPD give an edge of authority and make *The Perfect Teacher Coach* an essential tool for a busy teacher – not something additional or optional.

Elanor Westbury,
SENCo and English Teacher, King's Lynn Academy

An excellent, easily digestible guide to coaching in education settings, rooted firmly in the current climate of accountability and extraordinary expectation. This book navigates a path through the minefield of performance management whilst supporting a culture of humanity. Without emotionally intelligent leadership, schools and colleges act as dubious role models not only to staff but also to young people. Coaching supports high quality professional development and leadership in a way that excites and inspires those who learn and work in the organisation. *The Perfect Teacher Coach* is appropriately rich in addressing these issues and practical in supporting the implementation of high-end coaching.

Will Thomas, Performance Coach and
award-winning and best-selling author

A must for any head teacher looking to use coaching to enhance their school improvement journey. Coaching must be part of the school's culture for continuous improvement. Some great tips for all staff, teachers and teaching assistants looking to embark on the role as a coach. Great top tips – I will be using these with all my staff.

Eliza Hollis, Executive Head Teacher, Stoke Bruerne, Tiffield and Whittlebury Primary Schools

A well-structured, focussed and informative read, which still manages to maintain a conversational and highly enjoyable tone! Interspersed with opportunities to reflect on personal practice and to experiment with coaching techniques, the authors balance research, up-to-date educational practice and points of introspection extremely well.

I found myself nodding along in total agreement, furiously making notes on what we could immediately implement in school. The short plenary sections at the end of key chapters focus thinking and the carefully-worked examples are easy to follow and emulate.

This book puts into clear language the nuances and central essence of effective coaching within a school context, whilst maintaining a realistic and pragmatic understanding of school systems, performance management and school improvement.

I would heartily recommend this book to anyone embarking on coaching work for the first time or, equally, the experienced teacher-coach who wishes to re-articulate, consolidate, develop and reflect on their own personal and institutional practice.

Elizabeth Barratt, Teaching Coach,
The Nottingham Emmanuel School

An excellent teaching and learning guide for prospective coaches, with step-by-step guidance and information about coaching. *The Perfect Teacher Coach* clarifies the differences between counselling and coaching and the importance of good feedback from colleagues and fellow coaches. It provides a great way of reflecting on performance and management, questions the methods and ideas that we use within the classroom and structures coaching conversations.

Hayley Lockey, SEN Teaching Assistant and
advanced coach, Kings Lynn Academy

As a school we are certain that coaching is an incredibly powerful tool in teacher and student learning. Jackie provides a book that is easy and clear to read, just like *The Perfect Ofsted Lesson/Inspection* and that covers the basic premises behind coaching as well as developing strategies. The way the book is written creates a positive mindset for the reader in imagining what they might do in a particular situation. The wealth of suggestions and solutions coming from real examples and scenarios provides a real grounding for the skills that it develops. The chapter on questioning was one of the best that I have read - it provides clarity around the types of questions and when and where they are best used. It also makes coaching look easy!

This book very cleverly made me realise that I often coach effectively and that this happens when I have genuine empathy with the coachee. It has also given me the confidence to think beyond a prescribed set of coaching questions as I develop my coaching still further.

This is a book that will support the development of coaching skills in all teachers, young or old, experienced or NQT, but it also highlights the importance of coaching skills in support staff and teaching assistants. A thoroughly enjoyable and informative read.

Phil Loveday, Head Teacher, Bridgnorth Endowed School

# THE PERFECT COACH

teacher

Jackie Beere and Terri Broughton
Foreword by Vic Goddard

**i** Independent Thinking Press

First published by
Independent Thinking Press
Crown Buildings, Bancyfelin, Carmarthen, Wales, SA33 5ND, UK
www.independentthinkingpress.com

Independent Thinking Press is an imprint of Crown House Publishing Ltd.

© Jackie Beere and Terri Broughton 2013

**British Library Cataloguing-in-Publication Data**
A catalogue entry for this book is available
from the British Library.

**Print ISBN 978-1-78135-003-4**
**Mobi ISBN 978-1-78135-024-9**
**ePub ISBN 978-1-78135-025-6**

Printed and bound in the UK by
Gomer Press, Llandysul, Ceredigion

## For Tony, Amy and Sam

Thank you for consistently showing me patience, sincerity, passion, enthusiasm and love. You are my world!

Terri

---

## For Lucy, Carrie and Kirstie

Thanks for bringing us so much fun and happiness ... and showing us the real meaning of teaching and learning ... and coaching. I am looking forward to the next generation, in eager anticipation of more of the same.

Jackie

# Contents

# Acknowledgements

We would both like to acknowledge everything we have learned from all the excellent teachers and leaders we have worked with over the years, and the trainers and coaches who have inspired us – especially Andy Vass, Will Thomas and Mike Hughes. We particularly wish to thank the staff and students at King's Lynn Academy, Attleborough High School, Rawlins Community College, Swaffham Hamond's High School and Campion School who have supported and inspired us and all the individuals who have been willing to take the risk of making a change and doing things differently. Thanks also for the patience and commitment of our wonderful publishers, particularly Caroline Lenton at Crown House Publishing.

Special thanks must go to the coaches from King's Lynn Academy and from Swaffham Hamond's High School (now the Nicholas Hamond's Academy) for giving permission to use quotes from them throughout the book.

Most of all, thanks to our husbands for their unstinting support, particularly for the many hours spent by Jackie's husband, John Beasley, sorting out our ideas through his genius editing and for giving us the confidence to complete this book.

Jackie Beere and Terri Broughton

## A personal note from Jackie:

I would like to thank Terri. Some years ago she asked me to be her coach and my response was 'What do you mean?' After working with her, I now believe coaching is simply the most effective way to support and grow our fantastic teachers to be the very best they can be in today's high-stakes, judgemental climate. I have learnt so much from Terri about the ways she has used coaching at her school and in how she conducts her life. Thanks, Terri.

# Foreword

The 'Perfect' series is making quite a name for itself in my school. We have excitedly ordered each as they have come out and the staff have taken real comfort in the support they have been given. So I am really flattered to be asked to write the foreword for *The Perfect Teacher Coach*.

Coaching has been a buzz word in education for many years but I am not certain how successful it has been on a wide scale because teachers have spent far too long telling people what they need to do to solve a problem. Let's be honest, within ten seconds of someone coming to get support for something that is challenging them we, as teachers, have normally assessed what we think they need to do and all we are waiting for is for them to pause for breath so we can jump in and tell them what they need to know and do! We are busy people and we think that this will let us get back on with our own work. However, anyone that truly under-stands coaching and what it can do realises that actually the person you have helped will soon be back with a similar problem as they want the comfort of being told how to solve it. This absolves them from responsibility, to some degree.

As a Head Teacher, I have long since learned that trying to 'convince' anyone that coaching is something they can benefit from when they don't really know what coaching is leads to extra stress – and a lot of moaning in the staffroom.

What *The Perfect Teacher Coach* does is to clarify what coaching is and its power. Having worked hard to introduce a coaching culture in my own school, the hurdles have always been to make sure staff don't confuse coaching with something much more fluffy! So if you are dubious about coaching, just reading Chapter 1, that clarifies the differences between coaching, mentoring, counselling etc, will help you decide whether you have the skills and patience to be a great coach – not everyone does.

Like all of the 'Perfect' series, the honesty with which it is written means that anyone can pick it up and not feel they are being 'sold' something. There is little doubt that we are in a time of great change and increased pressure at all levels of our profession and the development of a 'growth' mindset is vital for any of us to cope. What this book delivers, that so many other coaching 'manuals' don't, is the links drawn with the things that are causing lots of us stress – Ofsted, performance management and becoming an outstanding teacher, to name a few of the 'biggies'!

As someone that is coached by a member of staff within my own school, a learning support assistant when I asked her to help, I know how much I have been supported by her skilful listening and questioning. It works and it helps me be better at the job I love. Coaching is non-hierarchical and non-judgemental – that is quite hard to find in our jobs currently!

The bottom line for all of us, as teachers and leaders, is that we want to make long-term and sustainable improvement for those that we work with – students and colleagues alike. The almost step-by-step guidance given allows anyone to take on the coach role if they want to. This book certainly explains the important skills and attributes we all need and has given me a new term to use with staff – 'owning the change'. In a nutshell, that is what coaching does and that is what this book helps you to accomplish.

Vic Goddard, Principal, Passmores Academy, Essex

## Introduction
# Who this book is for

All teachers 'coach' each other and their pupils every day in various ways. The 'perfect' teacher coach will use the powerful techniques described in this book to be the very best teacher, learner and coach that they can be.

This book is for anyone who:

- ▦ Is committed to whole school improvement and achievement.
- ▦ Is looking for sustainable personal and professional support.
- ▦ Cares about creating the best working environment for their staff and raising their morale.
- ▦ Wants their students to have access to the best quality teachers.
- ▦ Understands that one size does not fit all and that coaching is an opportunity to have differentiated support.
- ▦ Would like to encourage healthy, collaborative teams working together towards the same targets.

- Understands that there is more than one way to solve problems.
- Enjoys learning and practising new skills.
- Wants personalised learning for staff and students.
- Wants to develop independent, critical thinkers.
- Wants an empowered workforce with staff and students alike feeling valued.
- Wants to encourage participation, comment and feedback from staff.
- Has a vision of a school where teachers own their own progress and self-improvement.

Coaching is a term widely used in both the public and private sectors but it is also frequently misused and misunderstood. Yet true coaching, properly used and understood, has a remarkable impact on both individuals and organisations. Coaching should be part of your 'growth mindset' leadership strategy as a teacher, or as a middle or senior leader.

We strongly believe that it is inherent in human beings to want to continue to learn, improve and progress. Our hope is that this book will give you clear, focused and direct access to coaching skills that will dramatically improve both your own and your colleagues' practice – and encourage you to find out more about coaching. Our aim is to help you and other leaders develop and foster the reflective, emotionally intelligent mindset necessary to ensure continuous improvement for everyone in your community.

> 'Given the choice between someone with the desired mindset who lacks the complete skill set for the job, and someone with the complete skill set who lacks the desired mindset, a total of 96% of the employers surveyed picked mindset over skill set as the key element in those they seek and retain.'
>
> (Reed and Stoltz, 2011: 7)

This book is intended to help you develop a growth mindset in others by helping you become an accountable, approachable, listening and supportive teacher coach – with an understanding of key terms and skills inherent in the progression and support of colleagues and students. It does not profess to make you into the finished article by the time you have reached the final page. This is the beginning of the journey!

The book includes the latest expectations from the Department for Education and Ofsted, many of which can be met if you create a truly inspirational coaching culture, which in turn will embed sustainable personal and professional growth and transform your school. Above all, we want this book to provide you with some practical strategies to try out in your school, so that you can use coaching effectively to help support your teachers and improve learning for your pupils.

We also hope the book will clarify some of the key issues around coaching:

- What it is and what it is not.
- What the benefits are of developing the skills of coaching in your learners, your colleagues and your classrooms.
- How it can help you to improve the quality of learning for teachers and pupils in your school.
- How it can be successfully used in your classroom and with colleagues.
- How you can create a coaching culture that revitalises performance management, continuing professional development (CPD) and staff well-being.
- That it is best if used to personalise and differentiate support for teachers and then help them to own their own professional reflection and progress.

We also intend to show that coaching works to help you to:

- Balance challenge and support for your teachers to help make them the best they can be.
- Motivate and inspire your teachers to want to make progress.
- Support that long-serving, hardworking teacher to improve exam results with his/her challenging middle-ability groups.
- Help all your teachers embed high expectations in the classroom so that 'teaching and learning' becomes outstanding in your next inspection.

## Exercise

List what you think are the key skills of a coach – at some times in our lives we'll all have had an experience of feedback from an observed lesson or maybe we have been coached.

Consider a good experience you have had of feedback/coaching.

Consider a bad experience you have had of feedback/coaching.

Write a list of the behaviours that were helpful in achieving success.

List the behaviours that hindered your success.

Consider any feelings you had during this activity (whether expressed or not).

Given the same task on a different occasion, what could have been different/better?

---

The account below is a true story – investing in coaching can deliver such results.

## Send me on a course!

A middle-aged science teacher, with 15 years of teaching experience, said:

*'I didn't want this coaching thing. Initially I wasn't interested – I just wanted to go through threshold. I'd heard from others that it worked but was sceptical, however I decided to give it a go. Initially I found myself telling my coach to stop mirroring and matching me – I thought I knew what she was doing because I had worked in industry and was used to this type of approach. I found myself thinking: just send me on a course!*

*However, after a very short space of time I found myself looking forward to my regular sessions. My students were relating to me in a different way and I found myself enjoying my teaching more. I was able to notice things in a way that I hadn't noticed before. I came up with several different ways of approaching my 'lively' Year 9 class and very soon they were far more engaged in their learning.'*

Within two terms this teacher had changed her mindset about her pupils, her job and her expectations. It was highly noticeable to others – she had a smile on her face, was relaxed around colleagues and confident in dealing with pupils. She even seemed to quite like them now! She looked healthy and happy.

She went through threshold and became a secure 'good' teacher.

# Reflection

Before you begin your journey ask yourself the following questions – and be prepared to revisit them throughout the pages of this book:

- If you set yourself a target as a result of picking up this book what would that target be?
- How will you know that you have achieved it?
- What will you see, hear and feel having achieved it?
- What can you personally do towards achieving this goal?
- By when do you want to achieve it?

If you are a middle leader:

- What change initiatives have your teachers been involved with already?
- What is working well?
- How do you know?
- What abilities and skills do you already possess that will support you in bringing about a culture of coaching in your own school?
- What would need to happen for you to know that reading this book is time well spent?

# Chapter 1

# What is coaching?

*If you want one year of prosperity, grow seeds. If you want ten years of prosperity, grow trees. If you want one hundred years of prosperity, grow people.*

Chinese proverb

*I never cease to be amazed at the power of the coaching process to draw out the skills or talent that was previously hidden within an individual, and which invariably finds a way to solve a problem previously thought unsolvable.*

John Russell, Managing Director,
Harley-Davidson Europe Ltd

*You cannot teach a man anything. You can only help him discover it within himself.*

Galileo

Coaching[1] has been widely used in industry, sport and politics to support personal and professional development. It is the powerful process of supporting someone to move forward towards their goal. It is not a passing fad but is here to stay and, when it is done well, it can transform the culture of a school and empower teachers to respond positively to the relentless demands of continuous school improvement.

'Coaching is a highly structured way of working one to one with an individual through a series of meetings. The coach will enable the learner to take responsibility for his/her learning, develop an awareness of his/her situation and increase his/her skills. It is a way of reaching the potential of all staff.'

(Tolhurst, 2006: 3)

---

[1]  The origin of the word *coach* derives from the Hungarian word 'Kocsi' – the name of a town where horse-drawn vehicles were once built. The word then became associated with tutors who carry or guide students along a path of study. An alternative origin goes back to a time when wealthy families took their tutors with them in their coaches when they travelled and were 'coached' in various subjects on their journey. See https://teacherspocketbooks.wordpress.com/tag/origins-of-the-word-coach/ (accessed 7 January 2013).

'[Coaching is] a process that enables learning and development to occur and thus performance to improve. To be successful a Coach requires a knowledge and understanding of process as well as the variety of styles, skills and techniques that are appropriate to the context in which the coaching takes place.'

(Parsloe, 1999: 8)

In practice, coaching is a discussion, or series of discussions or structured conversations, which:

- Are highly motivating for the coachee.
- Use skilful questioning to identify issues.
- Facilitate learning and commitment from the coachee.
- Encourage the coachee to take responsibility for their actions and outcomes.
- Give choice about the content and direction of the discussion.
- Allow creative solutions to problems to emerge.
- Lead to clear targets and definite commitment by the coachee to agreed courses of action.
- Promote personal and professional development.

## What coaching is not

- Coaching is not a fluffy, cuddly, open-ended process that takes hours.

■ Coaching is not telling somebody what to do or showing them better/different practice.

■ Coaching is not rubbing someone's back and telling them that it will all be fine and agreeing that their classes are a real pain.

■ Coaching is not about continually analysing what went wrong but looks for practical solutions.

■ Coaching is not a one-size-fits-all process.

> 'Coaching has helped me to become a better teacher, leader and mother.'
>
> Liz Bernard, Advanced Coach

## A brief introduction to coaching

The terms training, mentoring, counselling and coaching are often, wrongly, used interchangeably but, as the table below shows, they are quite different. Each offers an approach that has its place depending on individual circumstances. We should always make sure that we use the right approach at the right time.

| Training | Mentoring |
|---|---|
| Passing on information, skills, knowledge and experience | A mentor will have had a similar role to the mentee at some point and: |
| Instructing | Shares their experience and expert knowledge |
| Telling | |
| Presenting solutions | Positively shapes the mentee's values and beliefs |
| Outcomes are delivered by the training | Gives specific advice and guidance |
| | Asks open and challenging questions |
| | Gives feedback |

| Counselling | Coaching |
|---|---|
| Helps people overcome their problems | Coaches work alongside their coachee to set clear goals and help to achieve them |
| Tends to focus on past issues with a view to moving forward | Is concerned with enhancing performance |
| Discovers the root cause(s) of long-standing issues | Is a two-way process which encourages the coachee to become a reflective practitioner |
| Looks for reasons why we behave as we do | Asks open and challenging questions which centre around what the coachee would like instead |
| Believes that individuals hold the answers | |
| Focuses on feelings | Solution focused |
| Solution focused | Action orientated |
| Advice not given | Addresses aspirations, objectives and tasks |
| Often used to diagnose and help with emotional problems | Structured approach |
| | Believes that individuals hold the answers |
| | Encourages the coachee to accept responsibility for progress |

In a school setting, we are likely to dip in and out of several of these approaches with staff or pupils. It is important to remember that these approaches can be adopted with an individual, a team or an organisation.

Coaches should always encourage their coachees to become more aware of and gain a greater understanding of their strengths and weaknesses in order to help them get better results. The approaches we use to accomplish these results sit along a continuum from 'directive' advice to 'non-directive' listening to understand (Downey, 2003).

> 'My coaching experience has impacted on and enhanced my ability to fully listen to concerns raised by my peers and discover approaches which encourage development and self-directed improvements whilst also holding staff to account for the decisions that they have chosen to make.'
>
> Amy Lee, Advanced Coach

## The coaching continuum

One end of the directive–non-directive continuum suggests that the person directing the conversation knows all the answers and will push the coachee towards them. At the other, non-directive end, the coach assumes that the coachee already has the answers, even if they don't know it yet, and that they can be drawn or pulled out and explored. Everyone

| DIRECTIVE (Push) | | NON-DIRECTIVE (Pull) |
|---|---|---|
| Giving advice<br>Instructing<br>Telling<br><br>**Solving the coachee's problem for them** | Making suggestions<br>Giving feedback<br>Offering guidance | Listening to understand<br>Reflecting<br>Summarising<br>Asking questions that raise awareness<br><br>**Helping the coachee to solve their own problem** |
| Trainer<br><br>Whilst this is sometimes called 'directive coaching' it is far more like training.<br><br>The trainer/instructor holds the knowledge which is imparted to the learner. | Mentor<br><br>The mentor has expert knowledge or experience and specific advice is given.<br><br>A good mentor may use elements from across the whole continuum. | Coach<br><br>The coach does not have to know the subject. She will be totally present in the here and now when working with her coachee and will |

| | | |
|---|---|---|
| encourage them to be totally present too.<br><br>The coach will use questions, enquiry and reflection in order to support the coachee to:<br><br>■ Uncover the issue for themselves<br>■ Explore their own resources, qualities and skills<br>■ Bring out the coachee's own potential<br>■ Raise awareness and give responsibility to the coachee<br>■ Encourage ownership of solutions by the coachee<br><br>The coach does not provide advice or refer to their own experience. | Effective mentors combine and blend suggestions with open and challenging questions. | Outcomes are delivered by the trainer. |

in a leadership role of any description should be aware of where they would instinctively be along this continuum.

Not surprisingly, many teachers tend to naturally err towards the directive/push end of the continuum!

Now look at the table below and be honest with yourself about which behaviours you would naturally tend to exhibit in a coaching (or a classroom or leadership) situation:

| Directive (push) behaviours | Non-directive (pull) behaviours |
| --- | --- |
| Directing | Asking questions |
| Telling | Testing your intuition |
| Instructing | Summarising |
| Giving advice | Paraphrasing |
| Sharing experiences | Asking the learner to summarise |
| Challenging assumptions | |
| Highlighting contradictions | Reflecting |
| Giving feedback | Listening to understand |
| Making suggestions | |
| Offering guidance | |

Adapted from Downey (2003)

# Trainer

It may be more accurate to describe 'directive' behaviours as training or instruction. The implication is that the knowledge is held by the trainer and is imparted to the learner by telling them how to do it (e.g. 'Here is how I would do this …', 'Here are our objectives …'). Trainers often point to their superior expertise and experience, but there is nothing worse for a coachee, after admitting a problem with a particular class, than to hear a trainer say how brilliant they are with them!

There is a place for directive coaching – sometimes we do need to say, 'This is how to do it!' But is this really coaching? Does telling the coachee how to facilitate their growth and self-awareness truly help them change ingrained habits?

# Mentor

A mentor will combine areas from across the continuum, freely giving hints and tips on how to improve – but will also provide a combination of open and challenging questions. The mentor may be a senior leader in the school or simply someone who has more experience than the coachee to whom they can pass on their knowledge.

# Coach

'Non-directive' coaching behaviours allow the coachee to take responsibility and require the coach to keep their own experiences at the back of their minds. A coach will, at all times, focus on the coachee's strengths and use them to support the coachee in achieving their goals.

The coach will not advise or direct but instead will listen, ask good questions, reflect, use enquiry and challenge, and encourage the coachee to take ownership and find their own solutions. This really is personalised learning at its best.

Some coaches describe this as being totally 'present' with the coachee and encouraging them to be totally present with you. When that level of trust is established, solutions to problems which neither you nor the coachee would have thought of previously will emerge.

At times, a coachee may want to invite suggestions from their coach, but should feel free to reject unhelpful ones and accept the most useful. If a coachee invites advice then it is perfectly OK for the coach to give it. The coach may ask for permission to do this at the beginning of the coaching session. Also, if the coach offers several ideas, the coachee can freely accept or reject them and still remain in rapport with the coach. For example:

**Coach:** *If I have some examples to share with you from my own teaching, is that okay with you?*

**Coachee:** *I'm happy to listen to new ideas but I may not be able to use them in my classes if I don't think it could work for me.*

**Coach:** *What works best for you when you try something new?*

Once the coachee has chosen an idea they find useful the coach can return to non-directive language, such as 'How can you put this idea into place so that it is specifically appropriate to your situation?' But if, for example, a newly qualified teacher (NQT) needs to find a particular policy document, it isn't very helpful for a coach to ask, 'Where do you think it might be?' A coach will move along the continuum depending on the situation before him/her.

The pattern of language and the tone of voice the coach uses are vital in gaining rapport with a coachee. This can make the difference between the coachee feeling that they are being told what to do and feeling that they have a coach who is listening to understand and trying to build genuine rapport with them.

The importance of building rapport and effective, helpful questioning are described later in Chapters 2 and 5, along with the attributes of good coaches and the techniques they use.

The table below shows how you could apply the different roles in practice.

| Trainer | Mentor | Coach |
|---|---|---|
| Delivers a CPD session with the latest ideas on giving feedback to pupils. Inspires teachers by modelling best practice and creating new solutions to try out in their classrooms. | Shares ideas and shows ways that giving feedback can make a difference in the classroom in homework tasks. Guides and advises how practice can be improved. | Follows up a training session by asking questions about how the coachee liked the ideas and how they will use them in a specific way in their own classroom with certain groups. Asks which ideas most appeal and if the coachee has any other ideas to add to the mix. |

# At a glance

■ Coaching gives ownership of change to the person who is being coached.

■ Coaching helps develop sustainable improvement in classroom practice.

■ Coaching encourages staff to take responsibility and accept accountability for performance.

■ Coaching is underpinned by the principle that everyone has resources they can tap into to make personal and professional improvements.

■ Coaching works by the coach developing a good rapport with the coachee that establishes trust and mutual support.

## Chapter 2

# What makes a 'perfect' coach?

The perfect coach will be honest, kind, respectful, inspiring and influential because of her/his humility. However, the perfect coach is also relentless and efficient in moving their coachee forward under their own steam. This chapter really peels back the many skills and attributes of the perfect coach so that you can become the best coach you can be.

## Who can be a coach?

Not all teachers will want to be coaches and, in truth, not all teachers will have the temperament to be one. The skills and attributes of effective coaches – such as active listening, rapport building and effective questioning – are fundamental to coaching and will have to be practised on a regular basis. You might want to look again at the coaching continuum on pages 16–17.

# The attributes of a 'perfect' coach

To work successfully, a coach must have a set of dispositions, principles and approaches that, when demonstrated by her/ him, bring about high levels of commitment, responsibility and learning in the coachee. They include, from the outset, an understanding by the coach that coaching is:

■ A non-judgemental and non-critical approach.

■ A commitment to building rapport and respecting the coachee's way of thinking and doing.

The perfect coach also has to believe at all times that coachees have all the answers to problems within themselves and so, allied to this, coaches must:

■ Be free of their own agenda.

■ Suspend their judgement and inclination to give direction.

■ Believe that people can find their own next steps in their development.

■ Seek to build and maintain resourceful states of mind in coachees.

■ Recognise and point out the coachee's strengths, and build and maintain their self-esteem.

■ Observe, listen and question to raise the coachee's self-awareness.

■ Encourage the coachee to develop personal responsibility and accountability and to continually improve their performance.

▓ Enable the coachee to set their own goals, to identify actions that they are committed to and to assess their own progress.

Coaches must also have a temperament which allows them to:

▓ Be positive and always believe that there are solutions to issues.

▓ Believe that self-knowledge improves performance.

▓ Be totally present and in the moment with their coachee.

▓ Be authentic and congruent.

▓ Be prepared and willing to learn.

And, when necessary, coaches should:

▓ Challenge the coachee to move out of their comfort zone.

▓ Know when it is, and is not, appropriate to shift to the more directive end of the continuum.

Finally, they also must have the skills to:

▓ Make agreements about how coach and coachee work together.

▓ Facilitate exploration and learning for the coachee.

▓ Break down big goals into manageable steps.

▓ Respect confidentiality.

Adapted from Thomas and Smith (2004, 2009)

Coaches also have to understand that to work well, the coaching process has to be an agreement entered into freely and willingly by the coachee. In a school context, a willing agreement to be coached is a more holistic, solution-focused way of working than simply telling a teacher (or student) coachee what to do and how to do it. Coaching is a flexible process, meant to draw out the potential within each coachee, rather than 'teaching' them. It can use formal and informal conversations to draw out the resourcefulness of individuals and encourage improvement. Coachees are far more likely to take on board ideas and techniques if they are using their strengths and owning the process. So a specific mindset is needed — essentially that coaching is about holding more effective conversations with staff and students whilst supporting them to be the best they can be.

In their book *First, Break All the Rules*, Marcus Buckingham and Curt Coffman include a study conducted by the Gallup organisation which looked at what makes a great manager. One million employees were surveyed over a 25-year period and the researchers found that leveraging strengths increased performance more than remedying weaknesses. Does this sound familiar to you? How often in a school situation do we focus on the weaknesses of members of staff and try to 'fix' them rather than building on their strengths? We also all tend to be acutely aware of, and magnify, what is not going so well in our practice and minimise or overlook our strengths.

'I have had some really good lessons since my last coaching session. I have felt a lot more confident since we focused on my strengths and that has come across in some of my teaching. I still need to make some improvements with some groups, but I honestly believe that coaching has helped me to start making some really positive changes.'

Coachee feedback to coach, King's Lynn Academy

Good coaches presuppose that people (and groups of people) are not 'broken' and do not need to be 'fixed', and that they have all the resources and hidden strengths they need to solve their own problems. Good coaches have an attitude of possibility and potential and know that coaching is a powerful method of supporting coachees, assisting them to engage in a process of continuous professional and personal development. Coaches recognise that coaching can also encourage coachees to be independent, critical thinkers who are capable of learning and growing. At its best, coaching uses powerful questions that facilitate the coachee to find their own answers and take responsibility for them; that is, to have an internal locus of control.

## The locus of control

When something doesn't go to plan it's easy to blame something or someone else – the students, the time of day, that particular group, the syllabus, other staff, the lunch menu and so on. This is to take what's known as an *external* locus of control. The belief here is that something is happening outside of ourselves and therefore is out of our control. It is negatively affecting our ability to succeed and we can do nothing to change the current situation.

When we have an *internal* locus of control we are far more likely to believe that we are responsible for what is happening in our life and work. Successful people tend to have an internal locus of control. Take these examples:

- External locus of control: 'Until the management/ leadership sort out the behaviour in this school I won't be able to teach a good lesson', 'There's nothing I can do until I get the new resources', 'I'm never going to be able to meet the needs of my Year 7 group without extra help', 'I'm fed up of telling people about ...'

- Internal locus of control: 'I have an opportunity to really improve the positive behaviour of the pupils in my classes', 'Perhaps I could design this better', 'I could try my own ideas to help Year 7'.

Teachers are very good at sharing the successes of their students with them and others but are far less likely to share or celebrate their own successes. Could this be because they haven't felt sufficiently listened to in the past and look for an external locus of control? If this is the case, it would suggest that many teachers need some coaching.

When we feel successful we are far more likely to be motivated. A good coach will encourage coachees to focus on solutions and to take an internal locus of control. They will engage in an open, honest, curious and sincere dialogue, examining and challenging any assumptions they both might hold.

## The language of possibility

Coaches use the language of possibility, breaking through the coachee's limiting beliefs and language of certainty and absolutes. They encourage their coachees, guiding them on a journey from how it has been, to how it is now and leading eventually to how it could be. But many coachees begin the journey with an external locus of control and use limiting language like 'can't', 'never', 'have to', 'must', 'should' and 'ought to'. Coaches will challenge this mindset of negativity and encourage the language of what is possible: 'can', 'could', 'maybe', 'might', 'perhaps' and 'possible', as shown in the table below.

| Language of impossibility | Language of possibility |
|---|---|
| I can't do ... | What if you could ...? |
| I ought to ... | How could you ...? |
| I should do ... | How about ...? |
| I have to ... it's compulsory | Why not? |
| I have never ... | How could this be an opportunity for you to ...? |
| I am absolutely sure ... | |
| He always makes me feel ... | Who else could support you in ...? |
| It's traditional to ... | Is there ever a time when you do not feel ...? |
| That is just how it is | How could you use your imagination here to ...? |
| I have never done ... no one has ever done that | I am curious, according to whom ...? |
| We have always ... | What if you did ...? |
| | Can you try ...? |

Note that the language of possibility is couched in the form of questions. The conversation is non-directive and encourages the coachee to come up with their own solutions to problems – always using the language of possibility and in a curious tone of voice.

> 'If you think you can or if you think you can't you are right.'
>
> Henry Ford

Habitually using negative patterns of thinking will not support the resolution of issues and can become a self-fulfilling prophecy. Have you noticed that when we become focused on negative experiences we seem to attract more of them? The language of possibility uses questions to try to inculcate a feeling of having an internal locus of control, which opens paths to self-awareness, creativity and – yes – possibility.

## Good questioning

The language of possibility contains many questions. Coaches use non-directive questions to draw out the solutions to problems from the coachees themselves – which is vital in engaging the coachee. There is much more on questioning in Chapter 5, which is devoted solely to questioning, and Chapter 6, where we describe the iSTRIDE coaching model.

*Important note:* The tone of voice and the pattern of language used by the coach will make a large difference as to whether the coachee believes they are being told what to do (directive) or that the coach has been really listening to understand the situation (non-directive).

So, good coaches also need good rapport skills.

# Building rapport

To be an excellent coach you need to know how to build brilliant rapport with the person you are coaching. If you can establish rapport, then you will make an emotional connection with the coachee that will help them feel heard and understood and so buy into moving forward with you.

If you feel comfortable and at ease with your coachee and have mutual trust, you are far more likely to draw out the best results. It is really important that rapport happens quite naturally. If it is forced, then the coachee will know it and it will have the opposite effect.

Coaches should observe other people when they are in rapport. They will often match and mirror each other's body posture and make eye contact. They may begin a sentence with the same words or use similar gestures when speaking. You might hear them say that they feel as if they have known you for a longer period of time than is the case, or that you really seem to understand where they are coming from.

In some types of training coaches are 'taught' these skills, but if they are carried out badly by someone who is really 'trying' they can have an adverse effect. We cannot stress enough how important it is to *be genuine and transparent, with no hidden agendas, not to just look sincere*, so that your coachee feels valued and understood. Coaching is not about creating an illusion of rapport, it is about genuinely being in rapport. This requires empathy and a genuine desire to connect with your coachee and help them move forward.

On occasion you may be asked to coach a member of staff who might not see the need for it, who might well be asked to suspend their beliefs and see things from another perspective or even to experience a complete paradigm shift. This is all the more reason for them to be able to relate to and trust what the coach is saying, so that you establish this as a 'done with' process and not a 'done to' process.

Establishing good communication can mean the difference between a successful and productive session and an uncomfortable session. If you have natural rapport with your coachee then this is great, but there will be times when they may be more guarded. This means that you must be flexible and adaptable in order to make your coachee feel comfortable and communicative. You are responsible for supporting your coachee to relax and talk openly to you, so you must continually adapt your body language, tone, language, volume and pace to suit them. If you can be totally congruent with your message, and sincere with your coachee, then they will be able to move themselves forward in terms of their professional practice and performance.

## Building listening skills for becoming a 'perfect' coach

Active listening is the most powerful tool you have as a coach. This may take practice and effort because you will need to let go of your own thoughts and concerns and really concentrate on hearing what your coachee is saying.

When we are genuinely listened to, it can support us in finding a better understanding of our situation and support us in discovering new solutions. Truly listening to your coachee with the principal commitment of paying attention in order to sincerely understand their point of view – how they think and their vision on the subject – is a pivotal skill in coaching. Moreover, listening for what truly inspires, lightens up, excites and frees a teacher, pupil, middle leader, member of the senior leadership team (SLT), higher level teaching assistant, cover supervisor, parent or school governor is a skill that can be learned. It is about listening not only for what *is* being said but also for what *is not* being said and noticing *how* it is being said – what feelings and emotions are being expressed or withheld.

This will need practice – and is an excellent skill to encourage in pupils too.

## Whose agenda?

Try this listening activity with a partner.

Put ten buttons in a pot. Person A talks for three minutes about something they feel very passionate about. They are informed beforehand that they must not use the words 'yes' or 'no' when asked questions, but other than that they can speak freely about their passion.

Person B listens but is allowed to interrupt and tries to get person A to say the words 'yes' or 'no'. If person B manages to get person A to say the words 'yes' or 'no' they win a button from person A for each time they say this. If person B gets all ten buttons in three minutes they have won.

Discuss how it felt to talk about something you cared passionately about to a listener with an alternative agenda! This little exercise is good for demonstrating how important it is to really engage with the speaker and focus on moving them forward – not just ticking your own boxes!

---

According to Julie Starr in *The Coaching Manual* (2008: 86) there are four levels of listening: cosmetic, conversational, active and deep.

## Cosmetic listening

Have you ever had the experience of being with someone who was making all the right noises whilst listening to you, but you knew that their thoughts were clearly elsewhere? You can either carry on regardless, feeling slightly uncomfortable or, if feeling braver, stop the conversation by asking if they are listening to you.

We have all experienced routine responses to enquiries about our appearance and been given answers that are not really relevant. 'Do you like my earrings?' 'They look lovely,' he says ... from another room. This is an example of cosmetic listening which many of us will recognise!

At a superficial level the listener may well be nodding in agreement or smiling with the odd, 'I understand,' 'OK' or 'That's good,' but they are not really paying attention.

This kind of listening may well be satisfactory for drifting in and out of a television programme or a group conversation in a social situation, but it is totally inappropriate for coaching. There are times, of course, when we lose the thread of what the coachee is saying. If this happens, it is best to admit it and apologise by saying, 'I am sorry, I did not get that. Please can you tell me again what you were saying?' Be honest. This way the coachee will know that it is important to you to genuinely hear what they have to say.

## Conversational listening

This is a dialogue between two people. However, whilst the speaker is being listened to, the listener is focusing on their own experiences. In other words, the speaker may lead us to think of a time when we experienced something of a similar nature. For example, 'I have a real problem with 8K2.' 'I know, I've had that class and they don't sit still for me either.' Whilst the listener is making more of an effort than at the cosmetic level of listening, they are searching *their own* experiences in order to make sense of what is being spoken about.

At times, the listener will compose their reply in their head – even as the other person is still talking! Here the focus of the listener is on how they will respond to the speaker, not on what they are actually saying. At other times the listener may well be making judgements, forming opinions or beliefs about the speaker or about something they are saying whilst they are talking.

## Active listening

The active listener hears the speaker's concerns, goals, values and beliefs about what is and is not possible and remains focused on what is being said in order to fully understand. They will cut off their own agenda in order to truly pay attention.

The active listener will also begin to use clarifying questions to fully appreciate what is being said, and will paraphrase information and reflect back to the speaker in order to check their understanding of what they are hearing. However, it is important not to continually repeat phrases such as 'You feel that ...' or 'You are saying that ...' as this can become irritating; it is vital that there is a genuine dialogue between two people rather than someone trying to remember their lines.

During active listening the listener will turn off their internal chatter and remain focused on the speaker. They will begin to notice subtle changes in physiology, tone of voice and the words the person is using, listening out for examples of where the speaker's locus of control is located. In a coaching context, the coach may well jot down a few notes (with the coachee's permission).

## Deep listening

Coaching demands deep listening – allowing the coachee a chance to be heard. Julie Starr refers to deep listening as being unlike any other: 'I have heard people describe good coaches as "almost telepathic" because of their ability to listen and to understand another person from insights into what they have said, or even understand what they have not said' (Starr, 2008b: 91).

This is the state of energised, intuitive focus where the coach is fully involved in the process. This is known as a state of 'flow', a term first coined by Mihaly Csikszentmihalyi: '"Flow" is the way people describe their state of mind when consciousness is harmoniously ordered, and they want to pursue whatever they are doing for its own sake' (Csikszentmihalyi, 1992: 6). In this almost meditative state the coach is totally immersed in the moment with their coachee, with nothing else on their mind other than what the coachee is saying.

## The presenting problem and the underlying issue

All the listening strategies described above are designed to help the coach take the coachee on a journey. Along the way the coachee will realise – often admitting to themselves for the first time – what the causes of the problems they present with really are. Later chapters in this book outline in greater detail the skills of questioning that will encourage empathy and growth in teachers in your school as they connect with their own motivation and potential.

# Active listening tips

- Be aware of your own prejudices and perceptions.
- Keep your advice, opinions and assumptions to yourself.
- Summarise and paraphrase to show you are listening and keeping your full attention on the coachee – be present.
- Listen with your eyes as well as your ears – be actively interested in what your coachee is saying.
- Use empathy to place yourself in your coachee's shoes – how might they be feeling right now?.
- Keep the conversation focused on what the coachee says and not your own agenda.
- Spend more time listening than coaching (it should be a ratio of around 80:20).
- Don't dominate the conversation with your own thoughts and ideas – ask your coachee if they would like you to make suggestions.
- Pay attention – don't become preoccupied with your own thoughts by turning off your internal dialogue (that little voice inside all of our heads that gives a running commentary – can you hear it?).
- Do not complete your coachee's sentences.
- Plan your response *after* your coachee has spoken, not whilst they are speaking.

■ Ask clarifying and open questions.
■ Summarise.

The skills so far examined in this chapter have included interpersonal skills, essential listening skills and the skills of building rapport with a coachee. At this point it might be good to ask what coaches gain from coaching.

## What do coaches get out of coaching?

The benefits of becoming a coach are countless but include:

■ A positive impact on the coach's own well-being.
■ A feeling of deep satisfaction in watching others grow and develop.
■ A sense of success in having supported others to reach their goals.
■ Developing their own existing skills and abilities.
■ Continually adding tools to their skill set.
■ Supporting and developing their leadership role(s).
■ Engaging with others in teaching and learning.
■ Building relationships with staff and students.
■ Meeting 'the challenge' with another.

# At a glance

■ A perfect coach is an active, empathetic and deep listener.

■ Building rapport is essential for good coaching and it can only be achieved through openness and trust.

■ A coach allows the coachee to make progress through self-reflection, instigated by great questioning.

■ A good coach listens actively and deeply to the issues that the coachee is describing.

■ Coaches gain skills and confidence from the process.

■ Coaches must be non-judgemental.

■ Coaches need to believe that their coachee has all the resources within them to make progress.

43

# Chapter 3

# Coaching with edge, for performance management

Whatever the context of your school, one thing is for sure: the quality of the learning and pupils' achievement will depend on the quality and commitment of your teachers. The 2012 Ofsted framework puts the observation of teaching and learning at the very heart of school evaluation. Your school can only be as good as the teaching being delivered in lessons five hours a day, five days a week. 'Typicality' of the learning experiences for pupils in your school is the key criterion for inspectors' judgements. They aren't interested in a one-off, great performance but in the routine delivery that raises aspirations and determines good long-term outcomes.

Those of us who have led training for thousands of teachers can immediately tell which schools will embrace the newest strategies with flair, enthusiasm and confidence. Not all teachers think they can do this, but those that do become our trailblazers and often go on to be leaders. However, we must challenge and support *all* our teachers, whatever their characters and capabilities, to be the very best they can be and to deliver consistently good and outstanding learning.

In difficult circumstances we may find ourselves 'coaching with edge', a term coined by Shona Walton, Head of Warwickshire School Improvement Services.[2] This term reinforces the notion that coaching can provide the critical challenge so essential to school leaders and teachers if they are to foster a spirit of open self-evaluation.

As John Hattie outlines in his book *Visible Learning*, successful teaching depends on every teacher's 'mind-set', because great progress depends on teachers believing that they are 'change agents' (Hattie, 2011: 22). Effective teachers are also eager to know their impact, have high expectations for themselves and their students and develop an implicit language for learning (Hattie, 2011: 19). They are flexible and responsive to the needs of their classes and have the seven habits outlined by Jackie Beere in *The Perfect Ofsted Inspection*: optimism, empathy, flexibility, courage/resilience, collaboration, self-management and reflective practice (Beere, 2011: 16).

How can we help teachers in our schools develop these habits and also respond to them as highly demanding professionals who won't put up with second best? And how do we reach the teachers who really need to improve?

Each of the seven habits can form part of the coaching conversation as set out in the table below.

---

[2] Personal conversation with the authors.

| Optimism | What has been your favourite teaching moment this week? |
| | How can you see progress in your very best pupil? |
| Empathy | Which other teacher could you help this week? |
| | Describe one of your lessons from the viewpoint of your most challenging pupil. |
| Flexibility | How could you introduce your lesson objective in a novel way this week? |
| | Which of the following will you try this week: a new food, a different route to work, talking to a different person at lunchtime, starting a new hobby? |
| Courage/resilience | What new strategy are you going to try out to help your 'gap' pupils make more progress? |
| | What would you like to present for a seven-minute TeachMeet INSET next week? |
| Collaboration | What is your best idea you have shared this term? |
| | Who could you work with on a new project to extend your skills? |

| Self-management | How can you ensure you always start your lessons on time? |
| | What evening of the week do you make sure you relax? |
| Reflective practice | How are you going to ask your pupils for feedback on your lessons this week? |
| | What mini research projects would you like to complete? |

## Using performance management as a big stick to improve teaching

In the last ten years, appraisal systems have often been seen as little more than a paper exercise, often with limited effectiveness, and are sometimes perceived as arbitrarily imposing school priorities on teachers through their personal targets. Until recently, common practice meant that no one was even allowed to see the targets, apart from the head and a professional tutor. These targets were often negotiated in a hurried chat once a year and then put in a file to be dusted off as part of an annual review which had no teeth. So nothing changed. The targets weren't met because they weren't monitored and so, worst of all, no child benefited.

This had to change – and it has. Ofsted now demands that performance management is effective and expects leaders to take quick and decisive action with regard to incompetence, as well as to help teachers who are 'good' become 'outstand-ing'. This has encouraged heads to link the pay scale progression of some 'inadequate' or 'satisfactory' teachers and to use the 2012 Teachers' Standards to justify it (see pages 57–61).

But this won't help teachers who are struggling. They will feel disillusioned and demotivated by the process. It will not help them to improve their practice or deliver the very best learning. Neither will it help their pupils. Nevertheless, the pressure is still on from Ofsted who will now be reporting on whether performance management (including pay pro-gression) is delivering continuous teacher, and thereby school, improvement. But the performance management/appraisal process is still too infrequent and often too separate from the daily grind of teaching to be able to effectively impact on performance.

With the new performance management criteria in the 2012 framework, now is the time for senior leaders to consider how to build highly effective and engaging professional development that helps all teachers be the very best they can be. Successful schools are developing a multifaceted approach to teacher development, which includes developing a culture of reflective practice and the sharing of research, resources, schemes and ideas. The move towards CPD that is delivered in-house and differentiated to suit the needs of individuals ensures a connection between performance management and teacher development. In this context, coaching can be a core development tool to help provide the support required to implement new strategies that will work to improve pupil outcomes.

## Practical ideas for engaging professional development

- Breakfast swap-shops when teachers are rewarded with coffee and croissants to bring in resources before school and share them with their colleagues.

- Teaching and learning cinema: show a lesson a month for all to critique and assess using the school observation format. Compare grades and feedback to establish conversations about learning.

- Live learning INSETs where one teacher teaches a group of students in front of *all* staff. Teachers are then encouraged to critique the lesson in small groups and feed back in the plenary.

- Regular TeachMeets for local schools where all teachers prepare to present for two or seven minutes their latest successful (or unsuccessful) strategy for discussion.

- A range of mini research projects for *all* departments to sign up to on favourite topics such as feedback, questioning, homework, extended writing or oracy in the classroom. Each project results in a one side of A4 report on observations in the classroom against a context of international research and is presented to the staff (see Chapter 7 for more information).

- Develop a coaching culture with a team of trained coaches who coach individuals regularly according to need and lead training in coaching for all – including pupils[3] .

## Coaching in a school context

In an ideal world, coaching would not be about someone else's external agenda. When we are coaching, we want our coachees to own their journey towards improvement. The process has to be driven by something which the coachee wants to do. However, in a school context, the pressure is always on for all teachers to teach good or outstanding lessons and improve results – which many see as an external agenda, set by Ofsted and promoted by school management. In addition, schools are judged by the effectiveness of their performance management systems.

Coaching will be one of the ways a school manages and supports performance but, for it to be truly effective, coaching should be a supportive rather than a judgemental process. Encouraging teachers to be self-regulating and reflect honestly on their own performance is more sustainable for school improvement than solely using top-down targets. It is also teaching the teacher to model the very qualities of self-management that we want to see in our students.

---

3  Thanks to various schools for contributing these ideas.

## Top tips for making coaching supportive and getting buy-in from coachees

Any self-reflective teacher knows that there are ways in which they can improve their practice or expertise and that coaching may help them do it. So, in a school context, it is hard to think of an area in which coaching will not, ultimately, impact positively on classroom practice and so meet the external agenda. However, some coachees may initially need support to embrace the process, but they will do so if the school ensures that it:

■ Explains to all the purpose and benefits of coaching.

■ Establishes a clear vision for improvement that *all* buy into (see the seven habits above).

■ Ensures that coaches are skilled in making staff feel valued and acknowledged during the coaching process. This will demand proper training and appropriate coaches who have the skills mentioned in Chapter 2.

■ Gives staff confidence that the coaching process will support them to make progress and improve.

■ Supports a 'growth mindset' that values effort and believes that everyone can change and grow by learning through mistakes.

Coaching should always be first and foremost about meeting the expressed needs of the coachee – but in the end it will benefit the pupils and the school.

Both high support and high challenge are required for coaching to be successful in your school, as shown in the figure below. The challenge comes from having a shared vision that there must be the very best learning outcomes for all pupils. A safe environment, in which the coachee feels it is acceptable to discuss weaknesses and try out strategies to remedy them, is built through having trust in the process, backed by support from the coach and the school.

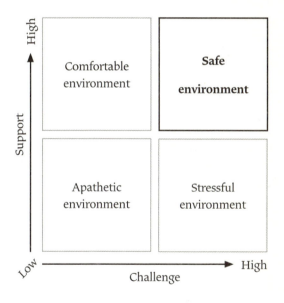

Coaching works, but, if you decide to use this powerful tool, make sure you evaluate the outcomes through quantitative and qualitative research (see the coaching evaluation tools in

Appendix 2). Ofsted have found that changes made through coaching in schools aren't always sustainable. The way to make changes endure is to embed coaching into your culture so that the change is not dependent on a few enthusiasts but permeates the way you do things at your school.

Coaching is personalised professional development that allows teachers to set their own agenda within the context of a powerful vision for school improvement. When a school embraces coaching, something special happens.

> Teachers find themselves talking to each other in a different way and feeding back to their pupils in ways that really support cognitive progression.

Here are a few examples of how feedback can generate thinking in different ways to encourage new solutions or ways of thinking in the classroom or staffroom.

| Written marking feedback | Coaching conversation |
|---|---|
| Your essay is rather descriptive and repetitive without getting round to answering the question. Use more key words. | What could you do to make sure you actually answer the question?<br><br>How can you ensure you don't repeat ideas?<br><br>What key words will be essential to include next time? |
| **Oral feedback on behaviour** | **Coaching conversation** |
| Your behaviour has been disruptive and unhelpful today and I want to see a more positive work rate tomorrow. | What happens when you behave at your best in lessons?<br><br>How can we both help that happen next time?<br><br>What would make you want to be a great learner? |
| **Staff advising each other on new ideas** | **Coaching conversation** |
| I find getting them to write a learning log as part of the routine before I get there has really helped settle everyone at the beginning of the lesson.<br><br>I always do the register in silence – that works for me. | What do you want to happen at the beginning of the lesson that would make you feel it is off to a good start?<br><br>What ways have you tried to achieve this so far?<br><br>What else can you try next time? |

The key is using questions to draw out the answers; this establishes more of a commitment to the solutions identified. Try it next time you give some advice – turn it into a question that probes their thinking and solves their own problem.

Research by the Sutton Trust (Higgins et al., 2011) shows that the most powerful and cost-effective way to improve progress for underachieving children is to give them feedback that helps them move forward in their thinking or skills. In fact, this study found that the top three, cost-effective strategies for improving pupils' progress were effective feedback, metacognitive and thinking strategies, and peer mentoring/learning.

All three of these strategies link beautifully with coaching as pedagogy. As teachers develop coaching skills, either as a coach or coachee, they experience the power of effective feedback and the strength of peer learning, and learn to challenge their own thinking strategies by reflecting on what works, how it works and what may work better.

The remaining chapters in this book aim to give you the tools and strategies to put coaching at the heart of school improvement – not as an add-on or latest wheeze to catch up on the gossip, but as the *relentless driver of self-improvement for staff and students*.

# Teachers' Standards, Ofsted and closing the gap

All schools know about closing the gap for pupils. But the gap between our highest achievers and those facing learning challenges exists not only for pupils but also for teachers.

> 'I'm assuming you've heard that Ofsted descended on us last week? ... I thought you'd like to know that we are out of Notice, having moved to Satisfactory, with almost half of the judgements being Good. Ofsted came in saying ... that coaching has made a tremendous difference to our staff – as did using the better teachers as role models for others. So, all the things [that coaching] kick-started over here helped us along the way.'
>
> Norfolk secondary school, 2010

The rest of this chapter will address how to close the gap between your highest performing staff and those bumping along in the 'just about competent' category. As mentioned above, most people are aware of their own areas for development, even if they are unsure how to improve them. Through collaboration with a coach, agreement about the need to change, and a commitment to it, can be made. Also, clear ground rules for how this is to be done, which are essential if forward movement and growth are to take place, can be put in place.

Coaching gives ownership of this change to the coachee. This is essential if change is to be sustainable. Coaches work from the premise that everyone has strengths which can be used to support areas for development. Language, particularly questioning, is used to draw out these strengths and encourage self-reflection and self-motivation to enable transformational change. This language is easy to learn and will looked at later in Chapter 5.

All but the oldest teachers will remember keeping a folder during training with evidence from their professional practice for all the standards. Teachers now need to demonstrate that they are meeting these standards 'regardless of their career stage' (DfE, 2012: 2). In addition:

'Following the period of induction, the standards will continue to define the level of practice at which all qualified teachers are expected to perform. From September 2012, teachers' performance will be assessed against the standards as part of the new appraisal arrangements in schools.'

(DfE, 2012: 3)

However, the school inspection handbook from Ofsted says:

> 'Academies are not required to apply the "Teachers Standards" as part of their performance management arrangements. However, inspectors should examine closely how the academy promotes high quality teaching through its performance management and professional development arrangements.'
>
> (Ofsted, 2012: 43)

So, entitlement to move up the pay scales depends on meeting the standards in schools or, presumably, closely related criteria in academies. Teachers have been used to having to find some evidence to pass through threshold but now schools' performance management processes must include a review of how teachers are meeting these standards.

The preamble to the standards says that teachers 'keep their knowledge and skills as teachers up-to-date and are self-critical; forge positive professional relationships; and work with parents in the best interests of their pupils' (DfE, 2012: 7).

Alongside the new standards we also have Ofsted inspecting the effectiveness of the school's performance management and promotion strategies. They expect to see evidence that schools are helping all teachers continually improve – especially if they are moving up the pay scales.

During an inspection, 'Inspectors should consider how effectively senior leaders use performance management and the school's self-evaluation to focus professional development activities' (Ofsted, 2012: 15). This should include:

> ■ 'the robustness of performance management and effectiveness of strategies for improving teaching, including the extent to which the school takes account of the "Teachers' Standards" – this is demonstrated through:
>
> - the robustness of procedures for monitoring the quality of teaching and learning and the extent to which underperformance is tackled
> - a strong link between performance management and appraisal and salary progression
> - the coherence and effectiveness of the programme of professional development, and the opportunities provided for promotion. Particular attention should be given to the extent to which professional development is based on the identified needs of staff and the needs of newly qualified teachers and teachers at an early stage of their career
> - the accuracy with which best practice is identified and modelled.'
>
> (Ofsted, 2012: 43)

They then paraphrase this and use it as a grade descriptor for 'outstanding' in the judgement of the quality of leadership in, and management of, a school:

'Leaders focus relentlessly on improving teaching and learning and provide focused professional development for all staff, especially those that are newly qualified and at an early stage of their careers. This is underpinned by highly robust performance management which encourages, challenges and supports teachers' improvement. As a result, teaching is outstanding, or at least consistently good and improving.'

(Ofsted, 2012: 46)

Leaders cannot simply direct all their teachers to become good or outstanding. They have to, as it says above, encourage, challenge and support them. This sounds like coaching will be required! An inspiring INSET session will provide ideas for some of your teachers to develop in their own classroom but others will need encouragement and support to make it work for their style and context. Coaching helps teachers make the most of that expensive training event by ensuring that new techniques are put into practice in the classroom at a pace and in a way that suits the teacher and the subject.

## How does coaching relate to 'outstanding' teaching?

The Ofsted grade descriptors for outstanding in the judgement of quality of teaching in the school include:

> ▪ 'Teachers systematically and effectively check pupils' understanding throughout lessons, anticipating where they may need to intervene and doing so with notable impact on the quality of learning ...
>
> ▪ Teachers and other adults generate high levels of engagement and commitment to learning across the whole school.
>
> ▪ Consistently high quality marking and constructive feedback from teachers ensures that pupils make rapid gains.'
>
> (Ofsted, 2012: 36)

All of the above can be enhanced with the coaching ethos by:

▪ Using coaching questions that support pupils in developing their thinking such as: 'How could you think about this task differently to make progress?', 'What do you need to change to improve your stories?', 'What have you done this lesson that will help you be a better learner?' (see Chapter 5 for an extensive list of coaching questions).

▪ Using collaborative tasks that encourage teamwork skills.

▪ Pupils setting their own success criteria that relate to the desired learning outcomes.

- Pupil-designed learning activities.
- Peer assessment and peer coaching.
- Reflection on the learning process and time for supported improvement of work.

## Using the Teachers' Standards in coaching

If teachers are to 'make the education of their pupils their first concern and are accountable for achieving the highest possible standards in work and conduct' (DfE, 2012: 7) they must meet a total of 35 standards under the following headings:

> - 'Set high expectations which inspire, motivate and challenge pupils
> - Promote good progress and outcomes by pupils
> - Demonstrate good subject and curriculum knowledge
> - Plan and teach well-structured lessons
> - Adapt teaching to respond to the strengths and needs of all pupils
> - Make accurate and productive use of assessment
> - Manage behaviour effectively to ensure a good and safe learning environment
> - Fulfil wider professional responsibilities'
>
> (DfE, 2012: 7–9)

As such, it makes sense to encourage all staff to continue to keep a professional portfolio under the above headings and use it for their performance management interviews. Simply keeping a note of pupil results, training sessions, sample lesson plans, feedback from parents or pupils and so on, updated as part of the performance management process, will give an opportunity for teachers to be self-critical about their strengths and weaknesses and help set appropriate targets for improvement.

## Where does coaching come into performance management?

The coaching example below shows a summary of a coaching conversation linked to performance management.

**Hint**: You might like to ask yourself these – and other questions based on any of the Teachers' Standards – *before* any performance management interview. You might also want to consider what you would use as evidence for your answers.

**Coach:** *What have you been doing to affect positive change in engagement?*

**Coachee:**

▦ *I've used much more engaging and varied starters.*

▦ *I've been using a 'hook' to engage the students.*

- *I'm more efficient by having less stress in the classroom.*
- *My students are becoming far more engaged.*
- *I'm much more willing to give ownership of the learning to the students and I'm still working on this area.*
- *I'm working on my plenaries – it's an on-going process.*
- *I'm very willing to take on board new ideas.*
- *I've been agreeing objectives with my students to enable them to take ownership of their learning.*
- *I'm able to show more enthusiasm for my subject to my students because I'm having to deal less with behavioural issues.*
- *I've been focusing on the process of science rather than only the facts. This makes a huge difference to my students.*

**Coach:** *What has been working well?*

**Coachee:**

- *The students are far more engaged.*
- *I use short video clips as a starter.*
- *The students are now writing 12-word Tweets to focus on the objective of the lesson.*
- *I give more time to helping individual students rather than dealing with so many behavioural issues.*
- *I have less 'call outs' from Student Support.*
- *I'm more aware of my voice tonality, body language and so on, and how the students respond to this.*
- *I take more time to reflect on my practice.*

**Coach:** *What has been challenging?*

**Coachee:**

- *The lateness of a few individuals sometimes disrupts a starter activity.*
- *There is still some difficult behaviour from a small number of individuals.*
- *A lack of confidence and low self-esteem in some students means they're still reluctant to attempt new activities.*
- *I've got difficulties with ICT access.*
- *Finding time during practical lessons for good starters and plenaries.*

**Coach:** *What are the positive learnings from these challenges?*

**Coachee:**

- *I'm focusing more on science processes and concepts and away from factual content.*
- *More time is available for one-to-one interaction with students.*
- *I don't allow a very small number of individuals to affect the learning of the whole class.*
- *Good starters now have a great effect on the rest of the lesson.*

**Coach:** *What is the next step?*

**Coachee:**

- *To make sure any starter activities are flexible enough for latecomers to join in with.*
- *To encourage risk-taking and new experiences for the least confident.*

- *To try to connect the learning even more with the real world to engage reluctant learners.*
- *I am going to build peer assessment into every lesson and reflect on what we learn from it.*
- *To ensure I have active, collaborative learning for at least 20 minutes in my lessons.*

Following a performance management interview, any target areas which emerge can be addressed through the coaching process. Coaching is, after all, a personalised process which can help teachers address their targets by taking positive action.

The conversation also gives an opportunity to follow up on progress through an observation, which can all be written into a simple coaching agreement like the example below.

**Date** 05/11/12

**Coachee:** Jackie Beere    **Coach:** Terri Broughton

**Focus for improvement:**

Using lesson objectives more effectively to achieve progress with Year 10 GCSE English.

**Action planned:**

Focus on specific objectives in all lesson planning using a variety of techniques from recent INSET.

Coaching observation on 15th November.

Obtain feedback from Year 10 students during December on engagement with objectives and progress made.

**Date for review observation** 10/1/13

**Signed: Coachee:**        **Coach:**

## Coaching observation example

Maths lesson: The coach is watching delivery of a concept then the pupils are practising exercises in pairs.

The coach tours the room checking understanding/work rate and feeding back directly to the teacher on which pupils need help or if a technique needs explaining again. The coach also advises the teacher on which pupils could come up to the front and demonstrate skills.

The coaching conversation during the lesson may start with these questions:

- ▨ Your delivery was clear and pacey – which pupils do you think are the most confident with this work?

- ▨ What could you do differently for those who are struggling?

- ▨ They have been working in pairs and a few are drifting off task. How will you check their progress in ten minutes?

- ▨ What are your strategies for John and Janet who have completed everything in double-quick time?

- ▨ What risky thing can you try next to surprise them?

- ▨ Do you think they still know the objective of the lesson? Does it matter?

These questions must be couched in a supportive and cooperative spirit so the pupils can see teachers working together to develop flexible approaches to learning. The coach is the extra eyes and ears in the classroom, who provides an extra dynamic to the lesson but also gives confidence for the teacher to try new things. This is essentially a non-judgemental observation intended to develop practice, not give a grade for the lesson.

This process and agreement can also be used as evidence for a performance management portfolio (electronic or hard copy) reflecting on practice and moving forward. This can be kept by the teacher along with records of self-assessment, coaching contracts, CPD/training undertaken, other professional development (such as mentoring NQTs), lesson observation feedback, action research projects undertaken, data on exam results and so on.

## Coaching observations for more targeted support

For a teacher with more pressing needs, a coaching session could include a coaching observation, which is non-judgemental but gives direct feedback, or coaching live in the lesson – whilst the teacher is teaching – in order to move their practice forward.

Too often feedback on an observation is delivered so long after the event that it is ineffective. A live observation encourages the teacher to be flexible and responsive as the coach can explain immediately how children are reacting to the delivery, thereby giving permission for the teacher to adapt the lesson in real time to meet children's needs. (See Chapter 3 for more information on this.)

## Getting pupil feedback

As you continue to develop your practice as a coaching school, you could include student feedback on the coaching agreement. This should seek out opinions from students about the specific improvements looked for and can be done either as an interview or through a questionnaire.

---

### Student Questionnaire

Please answer the questions carefully and honestly. For each question, please tick the box which best fits your response. Please ensure your tick fills only one box. Your responses will help your teachers to ensure that we offer you the best opportunities to learn.

**Group:**                            **Teacher:**

**Your gender: Male/Female (please circle)**

**Year group:**

**Thanks for your help.**

|  |  | 1. Never | 2. Sometimes | 3. Usually | 4. Always |
|---|---|---|---|---|---|
| 1 | Does the teacher share with you what you are going to learn in a lesson (the content and skills) at the start? | | | | |

---

| | | 1. Never | 2. Sometimes | 3. Usually | 4. Always |
|---|---|---|---|---|---|
| 2 | Does the teacher review with you what has been learned in a lesson at the end? | | | | |
| 3 | Do you have the opportunity to problem-solve with others in this lesson? | | | | |
| 4 | Do you have the opportunity to work as a group within this lesson? | | | | |
| 5 | Are you encouraged to find things out for yourself in this lesson? | | | | |
| 6 | How often do you get the opportunity to contribute in this lesson? | | | | |
| 7 | Do you know your current level? | | | | |
| 8 | Do you know how to get to the next level? | | | | |

| | | 1. Never | 2. Sometimes | 3. Usually | 4. Always |
|---|---|---|---|---|---|
| 9 | How often are you given the opportunity to review the thinking and learning you have done in this lesson? | | | | |
| 10 | How often does the teacher give you the opportunity to give extended answers in this lesson? | | | | |
| 11 | Are you taught to organise your thinking and learning in this lesson? | | | | |
| 12 | Does your teacher help you make links with other subjects as part of your learning in this lesson? | | | | |
| 13 | Do you have the opportunity to be creative (come up with new ideas) in this lesson? | | | | |

| | | 1. Never | 2. Sometimes | 3. Usually | 4. Always |
|---|---|---|---|---|---|
| 14 | Do you have a variety of learning opportunities in this lesson (do you do a range of different things to help you learn)? | | | | |
| 15 | Do you have the opportunity to try out new ideas in this lesson? | | | | |
| 16 | How much of the time in this lesson are you really challenged (really made to think)? | | | | |

This can be a powerful evaluator of the impact of coaching. If the aim is to find out how well we are doing in developing best practice, we need to ask the consumers of learning if it is working well!

See some further examples of coaching evaluation tools in Appendix 2.

# Chapter 4

# Creating a culture of coaching

## The challenge

Our challenge is to move all our teachers towards 'outstanding' along the continuum in the figure below – and that means working with individuals to address their own particular strengths and challenges. None of us is able to produce outstanding lessons all the time but our aspiration to be as good as we can possibly be, as often as we can, is an excellent role model for pupils.

| Inadequate | Need to improve | Good | Outstanding |
|---|---|---|---|

## Why coaching works – owning change

Coaching helps staff own the changes needed in their practice and actually take the required steps to action. It helps all staff take on board suggested changes in practice – and the helpful tips delivered in INSET – and gives them the tools to make them happen in the classroom through experimentation and implementation, and without feeling constantly 'judged'.

An appraisal conversation once a year setting vague targets – not owned, not clear and which never get monitored – will not instil a sense of continuous improvement. Neither will a prescriptive and controlling 'You will all create this weekly lesson plan and submit it to me by 9 a.m. on Monday' model. Staff development which works through fear, and which creates anxiety, will not create good reflective practice, sustainable improvement, self-critical teachers, inspiring teaching or outstanding learning.

Take, for example, embedding excellent assessment for learning into lessons. We all know that, done properly, this is one of *the* most effective tools for school improvement. Yet Ofsted research has found that it is not used well in many schools (Ofsted, 2008). Why?

If assessment for learning is introduced by having endless INSETs about it, delivered by strangers (or even the SLT), and by printing 'must do' tick-lists of strategies and writing them into the teaching and learning policies – disaster looms!

Without an understanding about how assessment for learning really works, and a belief in the hearts and minds of teachers that it truly benefits pupils, then it will not become part of their regular daily practice. So how can we help them believe that it will improve the process of learning in their classroom? By supporting them to try it out *properly*, learn from it and see that it works. And how do we do that? Through coaching.

## Coaching script

This is an example of a typical coaching conversation which could be part of a weekly coaching meeting or as a response to a teacher having a less than satisfactory lesson observation and being identified as in need of some support.

**Coach:** *How can I support you, Tony?*

**Tony:** *I have a problem with my Year 8 class. They will not pay attention to me and misbehave for the majority of my lessons.*

**Coach:** *Could you tell me a bit more about this class, Tony?*

**Tony:** *Yes. Other teachers tell me they are a hard class and I am at a loss as to how to control them. I try my hardest to do the best for them each lesson but this class are a nightmare! They don't listen and they all mess around.*

**Coach:** *Are you saying that the entire class are a nightmare each lesson, Tony, every student in the class?*

**Tony:** *No, not everyone. It is the ring leaders who spoil it for everyone else.*

**Coach:** *So the whole class is not a nightmare but some individuals are spoiling it for everyone else?*

**Tony:** *Yes.*

**Coach:** *Who are the ring leaders?*

**Tony:** *Lee, Mervyn, Matthew, Amy, Laura and Sam.*

**Coach:** *So, to be sure I am getting a clear picture of what you are telling me, are you saying that these six students are making it difficult for you to teach the whole class?*

**Tony:** *Yes, they make it very difficult.*

**Coach:** *Tony, has there ever been a time when these particular students have engaged in their learning?*

**Tony:** *Yes, odd times, especially when they are doing practical lessons.*

**Coach:** *How would you like it to be with Year 8? What would you like instead of what you have now?*

**Tony:** *I would like to be able to plan a lesson that they can all engage with and see clearly that they have learned as a result. At present this looks like an impossible task!*

**Coach:** *Going back to when they were engaged in the practical lesson. What was happening then that is not happening in their other lessons? What were you seeing then that told you they were engaged? What did you hear them saying? What were you saying to yourself at the time?*

**Tony:** *Lee often engages in a practical group session when I run them – he is strong and others follow him. I remember a lesson about three weeks ago when I really did think I'd done something right. These six students were engaged and the others in the class* *were able to get on as well. I remember being surprised because Amy and Laura were going to Lee for support and he looked like he was in his element. Even Mervyn, Matthew and Sam were engaged.*

**Coach:** *What strengths were you using at this time in order to get these results?*

**Tony:** *Because they were doing something they wanted to it made it easier on the others. As a result of this I was able to relax and give some responsibility to Lee. This led to the other five becoming more engaged.*

**Coach:** *If Lee is engaged are the others engaged too?*

**Tony:** *I had not thought about this before but the answer is yes. What is interesting is that I thought it was the whole group, but it isn't. It is the six students really but I have noticed that when Lee is engaged they look to him for guidance. I am unsure why this is but when Lee is engaged I am more relaxed. When I am more relaxed the class are more likely to engage.*

**Coach:** *What are the positive effects of engaging Lee in the lesson and you being relaxed?*

**Tony:** *If Lee is engaged I have a much better lesson – it runs far more smoothly.*

**Coach:** *I am curious, Tony. Are you saying that if Lee is engaged that the whole class are far more likely to be engaged in the learning?*

**Tony:** *Yes, if I am honest.*

**Coach:** *So what do you stand to gain by engaging Lee?*

**Tony:** *It is interesting because I came in thinking it was the whole class but I have realised that when Lee is engaged and motivated he will have a massive impact on my lesson.*

**Coach:** *So what have you learned so far?*

**Tony:** *That engaging Lee will make a big difference.*

**Coach:** *What does it cost you when you do not engage Lee?*

**Tony:** *It costs me my whole lesson and the learning of the rest of the class. Those five others join in with him and that is when I lose the class.*

**Coach:** *If you had a magic wand, if all restraints were removed and you could engage Lee, what would you need to do?*

**Tony:** *I wonder if I have a quiet word with Lee and involve him in my planning whether it would have an impact? I remember reading something that said, 'tell me and I will listen, show me and I will understand but involve me and I will engage'. I have not thought about that for years. I am wondering if I involve Lee and ask him to plan a lesson with me if it will make a difference.*

**Coach:** *Is there anything else that you could do?*

**Tony:** *I could see this class in other situations and look at how they respond. I could give responsibility to the other five students and see what happens. This would split the group up. I could give* *timed tasks and make the different parts of my lesson more explicit rather than rolling into each other ... my mind is racing.*

**Coach:** *On a scale of 1 to 10, where 10 is you are totally motivated to put one of your suggestions into practice, where are you at present and what would you like to put into practice first?*

**Tony:** *Actually I am going to give Lee some responsibility and break my groupings up. I am a 10 on motivation. I will go and see him later today.*

**Coach:** *What could the impact of Lee taking some responsibility have on the whole class?*

**Tony:** *Well, in theory it could have a massive impact.*

**Coach:** *So what is your next step, Tony?*

**Tony:** *I am going to see Lee in tutor time and have a word with him. I will suggest that he supports with planning some lessons and reward him for this. I think this will make him feel more positive.*

Coaching is the methodology for achieving the ownership of strategies for improvement. It has to be at the heart of all your training and tailored support for staff to meet the necessary standards and continually improve. Coaching has to be part of the wider culture in your school that says 'teachers are always lifelong learners'.

A structured coaching conversation (see the iSTRIDE model in Chapter 6) can lead to clear targets, exploration of issues, highly creative problem-solving and definite commitments to action. It is characterised by a set of principles and approaches that, when demonstrated by the coach, brings about high levels of commitment, responsibility and learning in the coachee. The staff themselves become the agents for change.

## Setting up and maintaining a coaching culture

The way forward for many successful schools has been to embrace coaching as a support process and as a way of securing change and development in behaviour. However, like all good practice, it has to be linked to the leadership vision and school culture and understood and implemented effectively to make a consistent, effective difference to teaching in your school.

A coaching culture means that rigorous demands about quality standards are accompanied by a supportive, open-door approach in every classroom and teachers are encouraged to be innovative and model the habits they want their learners to exhibit.

For coaching to work in your school (or any organisation) it has to be owned by the staff. Only then can it become sustainable. The culture has to be implemented systematically and deliberately in order to ensure that learning is shared and built upon, leaving nothing to chance. A good place to start is with the middle leaders.

# Leading the (middle) leaders

Middle leaders are key to the success of the coaching culture in any school – because they will need to do much of the coaching! It is vital that they see its benefits and buy into the culture. Some will need help and may need to be coached in their own role of leading a team and being held accountable for someone else's performance.

Some useful coaching questions to use with your middle leaders are:

- What are your strengths as a middle/faculty leader?
- What are your challenges?
- What skills do you need to develop?
- How are you developing them?
- What areas of faculty performance are you keen to improve?
- What do the pupils say about your faculty?
- How are you improving the performance of your team?
- What are your next steps for developing your leadership role?
- Where is your evidence for this?

Middle leaders need to be shown and convinced that coaching, properly implemented and carried out, is a better and more effective method for developing their staff than traditional performance management models.

# Case study: King's Lynn Academy (KLA)

Craig Morrison, the Principal of King's Lynn Academy, said in November 2011:

*'At King's Lynn Academy we offer coaching to all staff, teaching and non-teaching. The coaching model explicitly addresses the fact that in any school, even the outstanding ones, there are colleagues with very different needs and at different stages in their development. By using coaching as a professional dialogue, the school also models the more tolerant, listening approach it would wish to see used in interactions with students.'*

One size does not fit all and coaching seeks to target resources where they are needed and build trust on an ongoing basis rather than rely upon large training events which, by their nature, are impersonal and address a middle ground.

Where colleagues are not fulfilling their duties, a coaching dialogue can uncover the true emotions or motivations driving underperformance. The alternatives – taking disciplinary or capability action – are usually time consuming, expensive, threaten trust and rarely result in positive outcomes. Coaching is a high leverage strategy for reflection and improvement.

This figure shows how King's Lynn Academy is growing coaching to support the school community:

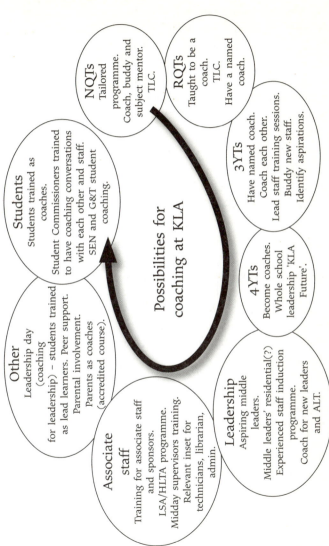

**Possibilities for coaching at KLA**

**NQTs**
Tailored programme. Coach, buddy and subject mentor. TLC.

**RQTs**
Taught to be a coach. TLC. Have a named coach.

**3YTs**
Have named coach. Coach each other. Lead staff training sessions. Buddy new staff. Identify aspirations.

**4YTs**
Become coaches. Whole school leadership 'KLA Future'.

**Leadership**
Aspiring middle leaders. Middle leaders' residential(?) Experienced staff induction programme. Coach for new leaders and ALT.

**Associate staff**
Training for associate staff and sponsors. LSA/HLTA programme. Midday supervisors training. Relevant inset for technicians, librarian, admin.

**Other**
Leadership day (coaching for leadership) – students trained as lead learners. Peer support. Parental involvement. Parents as coaches (accredited course).

**Students**
Students trained as coaches. Student Commissioners trained to have coaching conversations with each other and staff. SEN and G&T student coaching.

*Note:* NQT: newly qualified teacher; RQT: recently qualified teacher; 3YT: teacher with three years' experience; 4YT: teacher with four years' experience; ALT: Academy Leadership Team; TLC: Teacher-Learner Community; LSA: Learning Support Assistant.

At King's Lynn Academy, as in many schools, teachers needed to improve and progress their pedagogy. Coaching was introduced by a newly appointed leader of teaching and learning as a powerful tool for developing staff skills and ownership of change. She also introduced a programme of training with accredited coaching courses being offered (see below). Staff responded well to this initiative. For example, Geography teacher Peter Coote said:

'After 30 years of teaching, many spent in posts of responsibility, I found myself back as a classroom teacher and a little unsure of myself in the wake of an academy re-launch at my school. On the first morning, a new member of the team spoke to the staff about coaching. I was immediately engaged by the obvious passion [the coach] had for teaching and learning, but in particular I was interested by the picture she painted of how coaching could impact on our new academy. I felt that someone had somehow put into words what I believed in.

I made a conscious decision that morning to contact [the coach] and ask for coaching support. With the weight of responsibility off my shoulders, I was determined to revisit my pedagogy and aimed to make changes to my lessons which I hoped would make them more enjoyable for pupils and myself.

We set up weekly meetings and discussed a range of issues around my situation and what I wanted from coaching. The coach asked insightful questions and provoked a lot of thinking and soul searching, both during our sessions and between. I started trying a range of new approaches and the coach observed lessons, including taking videos of some of them, which we were able to watch back and discuss.

Initially, I was not confident enough to sign up for coaching training, but with support and encouragement from my coach I joined the group and took on catch-up sessions to fill in the gaps. I have committed to following the Advanced Coaching Award next year and look forward to coaching colleagues in my own right.

Some notes I wrote part way through the year about my experiences included:

*To stay aware of the responsibility to have an internal locus of control and to foster this in my students.*

*I notice that I am more relaxed and confident and that this has had a positive impact on my teaching.*

*I continue to make time to think about my pedagogy and to put new strategies in place.*

*I continue to feel positive and that things are moving forward personally and departmentally.*

I do feel more relaxed and confident that I can do this. I am comfortable with change and am enjoying the

> whole package of experiences which teaching provides. I am wholly committed to the coaching approach, as are several of my colleagues, and I particularly like the non-judgemental and confidential nature of the relationship between coach and coachee. My teaching is so much better!'

Later several staff, including teaching assistants, higher level teaching assistants and non-teaching staff, signed up to do the initial accredited Introduction to Coaching course (Institute of Educational Coaching accredited through Vision for Learning). Some of these staff have gone on to do the accredited Advanced Coach training. Teaching assistant Hayley Lockey, who is working with special educational needs (SEN) students and training them to use coaching language, said:

> 'Over the past two years training and working as a coach, I have worked with students and staff alike. This can be a five minute conversation in the corridor or a much longer planned, structured session. I've found coaching to be the one thing that gives staff the momentum to move forward and gives them the opportunity to make their own choices. It is a fantastic way of working along-side each other.

At present I am planning effective strategies to promote positive behaviour – this includes the links between learning and behaviour and the importance of support-ing pupils to develop metacognitive skills to support a solution-focused approach to developing positive learn-ing behaviours. My focus for this academic year will be to train our SEN pupils to use coaching language and to support one another.'

Laura Cowan, a deputy head teacher at Great Yarmouth VA High School, remarks on the benefits for faculties:

'Coaching has had great impact in our faculties and the staff have become noticeably switched on and excited by teaching and learning. Through this process, robust and thorough conversations are taking place which chal-lenge staff in a supportive and positive way.'

And Andrew England, head of organisational development at the College of West Anglia, King's Lynn, adds:

> 'We use coaching because it is the method that really engages staff and produces sustainable results. We are currently working with an experienced coach from KLA who uses coaching for improving teaching and learning, blending that with our coaching model which helps provide solutions to management problems.'

## Pupils as coaches

The coaching model of continuous improvement should evolve to underpin the school's approach to pedagogy. As teachers become experts at supporting each other, and their students make progress, they discover that a coaching approach and coaching questions (see Chapter 5) work brilliantly for pupils. As questioning and feedback techniques used with pupils improve, this helps pupils make greater progress in their skills and understanding and creates the classroom practice that will develop resilient, independent learners. Once you start coaching, you very quickly realise that the powerful, open-questioning techniques that help teachers own their own learning are the most useful habit to develop for helping pupils make great progress too.

The next stage is to train student coaches to have high-level peer support skills. Teachers in schools that use peer coaching find that it increases the quality of peer assessment, promoting better empathy and behaviour for learning. Why? Because coaching promotes a growth mindset which focuses on the process of learning (Dweck, 2006), as well as encouraging belief in a learning journey where making mistakes is just part of the process.

## Coaching as teaching and teaching as coaching

'In observing an excellent teacher at work recently, it was striking from very early on in the proceedings that she was clearly employing a coaching approach.

When a youngster asked a question it was, in effect, turned back to the pupil to explore and solve by means of specific questioning. This was never 'left in the air', but a focused interaction followed. The teacher-coach would only move away from focusing on the pupil if the youngster needed more time to process. She always left a door open for a return to further investigation with comments like, 'Well, you think about that for a little longer and when you're ready you can come back to me. All right?'

What was masterful was the way the teacher was using coaching methods. She never made her students feel threatened by demanding they must do the following task, but led them, via their strengths, to the desired outcome. For example, when a pupil believed he couldn't do a specific type of task, he was asked, 'OK then. What could you do to show this information?' He opted for something he could achieve and was then drawn out further by being asked, 'In what ways, specifically, do you think you could use what you've done to help you do this [the original task]?'

What was refreshing and exciting about this approach was that it was clear that the teacher was not only getting the pupils to learn, but to also differentiate between opinion and reasoned argument. As I discovered from talking to the pupils during the lesson, regardless of their academic abilities, she had helped them become both curious and reflective learners. This should be the aim of all teachers ... and it is a habit that will develop through experience of coaching peers and being coached effectively.

We would all do well to learn from [the coaching] approach to teaching and learning.'[4]

Chris Matson, education consultant, trainer and author.

[1]For a teacher to gain an 'outstanding' grade in their lesson, the 'gap' pupils, shown on the school data to be underperforming, must make outstanding progress. To do this, these

---

4   Feedback after observing a lesson led by a trained coach.

pupils need to discover new solutions and strategies to make learning work well for them. The best way to do this is to use coaching questions and feedback crafted to encourage cognitive development. This is a highly skilful role for any teacher – a skill honed by experiencing the power of good coaching for the teacher's own self-improvement.

## Observing lessons – coaching observations

There are many ways to observe a lesson. The Ofsted Inspection Handbook suggests short visits of a few minutes to a number of lessons, longer lesson observations of up to an hour and tracking a class or specific group of pupils across a number of lessons (Ofsted, 2012: 10). Ofsted observations usually involve triangulation of evidence about the teaching by talking to the pupils – especially gap pupils – and scrutinising work books. All of these are recommended as part of your school's performance management processes.

Official observations may be graded and recorded and any Ofsted inspection team will certainly want to see them. Records of observations (and actions resulting from them) will form part of the evidence of your own self-evaluation of the quality of teaching in your school.

Additionally, you may want to include 'coaching observations'. In these, the observer/coach is watching, listening and talking to pupils but during the lesson they coach the teacher, often (though not always) on a previously agreed aspect of pedagogy. When the pupils begin group work or are set on a task, the coach/observer gives instant feedback about what has been happening, holding a mirror up to the teacher about how the lesson is going so far. This is a non-judgemental process but it aims to help teachers become self-aware, responsive, flexible and to try out new ideas to help pupils make great progress.

Example questions in coaching observations might include:

- What do you think has gone well so far?
- Did you feel all the pupils were engaged in the objective?
- Did the pupils understand the explanation?
- How do you know?
- How is the pace for you?
- What could you improve now?

The questions provide an opportunity to reflect instantly on what is happening and enable the teacher to respond to needs/situations in the classroom which they may not have noticed without the help of the classroom coach. As this is not a graded, 'official' lesson observation it presents a chance for teachers to adapt their lesson and be flexible and responsive to pupil needs. This is especially useful for teachers stuck on 'needs to improve' Grade 3 and who are not sure how they can improve their lessons.[5]

---

[5]  Many thanks to Clevedon School, Bristol for their input into this section.

Chapter 4

# Grading observed lessons

In recent years, emphasis has been placed on the beneficial aspects of assessment for learning strategies where teachers don't grade pupils' work but give comments only, as awarding grades can become counterproductive (Wiliam and Black, 1998).

The same thing happens in formal classroom observations – many teachers wait to hear the grade they received for their lesson, concentrate only on that and then lose all the other feedback. Furthermore:

> 'It has been noticed in teaching that most teachers' experience of being observed is also that of being judged. This feeling, whether justified or not, tends to make people defensive and apprehensive about the process. This is not a healthy state for learning.'
>
> (DfES, 2003: 40)

This is why it is so important that the coachee is not in a position of being judged by their coach but enters into a two-way, trusting relationship, feeling able to discuss and develop their own practice. That said, the coach may well be in a position to challenge the beliefs and mindset of the coachee by asking curious, thought-provoking questions. It is far easier for coachees to take on board new ideas and concepts when they feel listened to and understood rather than lectured to. Good coaching also takes away the need for just one answer to the problem and allows the coachee to explore other avenues and possibilities. It is a process of growth and development for you as a coach, as a leader and as a member of staff.

## At a glance

- Ensure everyone knows how coaching fits into the vision for school improvement.
- Meet all teachers' needs and abilities by providing coaching delivered by well-trained coaches.
- Train all middle leaders to be expert coaches so they can help their teams improve performance.
- Use coaching to help all teachers progress to the next stage of their development by building in coaching sessions to their performance management programme.
- Use coaching observations to support teachers who need help with developing flexible approaches in the classroom.
- Make sure you allocate time for coaching to enable it to happen effectively (a successful coaching session can take just ten minutes but this can still result in a commitment to action).

- Senior leaders need to volunteer to be coached as well as teaching staff – this sends out a powerful message about how much you value the process.

- Ensure all staff have a coaching agreement/record sheet (see Appendix 1).

- Invite governors to take part in the process and train them in coaching if relevant.

- Monitor and evaluate your coaching processes and practice to measure impact and develop expertise.

- Encourage coaching techniques to be used by teachers, teaching assistants, pupils in the classroom.

# Chapter 5
# The skill of questioning

## Coaching questions

After listening, asking the right questions at the right time is the most powerful tool to support your coachee in opening up new avenues and possibilities. Children are brilliant at it! They show enormous curiosity and an enthusiasm to have their questions answered – but are often told to stop asking so many questions. It is this very inquisitiveness that a coach needs to foster, using different kinds of questions to suit different outcomes. When asking questions, coaches should use a curious tone of voice. Imagine a coach were asking you the following questions:

- If this book were to prove to be useful to you, how would you know?
- What would you be doing differently in your school?
- What else?
- Who else will know that this coaching book has been of use to you?
- What will they see you doing?

- What else?
- What will they hear you saying?
- What else?
- When will you know it has made a difference?
- How will you explain it to others?
- Where could it happen?

These are all 'open' questions and begin with 'when', 'who', 'how' and 'where'. They are designed to encourage discussion and a deeper level of thinking. A closed question like 'Is this book useful to you?' on the other hand will lead to yes/no limiting answers. No real detail is gained and deeper thinking is not required.

Coaching questions are powerful and need to come from a place of genuine curiosity and respect for your coachee, understanding that they already have the answers within them. Their purpose is to encourage the coachee to think beyond the presenting problem and get to the underlying issue, allowing the coachee to do most of the critical work so that they have ownership of the process.

To do this, the coach has a suite of questions to encourage self-reflection and which are able to move the coachee forward. The coach doesn't need to know all the answers but rather draws out ideas and solutions for a fresh approach from the coachee. Often the coachee will have tried to sort out the issue for themselves but have found that they are at a loss to know what to do next. A coaching approach here would be to question the coachee's frame of reference and encourage them to reconsider the way they define the issue: 'Have you thought of what would happen if you thought about this differently?'

This requires the coach to use listening, rapport and sensory acuity skills to be aware of how the coachee is responding throughout the session. Imagine having sensitive antennae that are highly attuned to every nuance of response in your coachee – their facial expression, eye contact, intonation and so on. Look relentlessly for clues to guide you about how they are feeling and how you can respond. Coaching is not about focusing on the problem as defined by the coachee but the way that they characterise the problem: how they see it and the way it makes them feel.

## Questions that encourage ownership

Carefully worded coaching questions which have the word 'you' in them can help to remind the coachee that they are responsible for their results. Remember, the idea is to encourage your coachee to take an internal locus of control:

- What would *you* like to focus on today?
- What results do *you* wish to achieve today?
- What is important to *you* in relation to that at the moment?
- How can *you* word that goal more specifically?
- How can *you* measure that goal?
- How can *you* break down that goal into bite-sized pieces?

- How can *you* word this goal using positive language?
- How do *you* want to begin this work?
- Where do *you* stand now?
- What could be *your* next step?
- How would *you* like to conclude this session?
- What strategies/ideas do *you* plan to implement before our next coaching session?

## Questions that draw out ideas and information

The purpose of questioning is to acquire new information or to generate new ideas. *Neutral questions* will support this:

- What is your perception of ...?
- How do you feel about ...?

*Open questions* increase the range of possible responses from the coachee:

- What do want to happen with that class?
- What options do you have?
- What could be your first next step?
- When would you like to have achieved this by?
- What would you like to focus on?
- Tell me something about ...

In this way the coach can get the coachee to open up and tell them about their work issue. Open questions are also used to help the coachee understand what they are there to

achieve and to reinforce the belief that the coachee has the
solutions.

## Questions that suggest choice

These questions suggest that there is an alternative or a
choice:

- Is this something you could do during your next lesson
  or do you need time to plan for it?
- Do you prefer option A, B or C?

## Practically oriented questions

Practical, pragmatic questions can help the coachee to focus
on specific situations. They are useful to ask at the beginning
of a coaching session and, along with follow-up questions,
will help focus the coaching process on solutions that can be
referred back to at the end of the session.

**Coachee:** *I can't seem to finish my lessons, I always run out of
time.*

**Coach:** *Can you give a precise example of a lesson that overran?*

**Coachee:** *I'd like to improve my relationships with my classes.*

**Coach:** *Starting with which class, to take a practical example?*

**Coachee:** *I hate it when people can't make their minds up.*

**Coach:** *Who, specifically, can't make their mind up?*

## How questions

How questions can support the coachee in visualising future possibilities (e.g. 'How will you ...?', 'How are you going to ...?'). The question presupposes that the coachee is ready to move into action. The question, 'How are you going to implement this new strategy in your teaching?' presumes that the strategy will be implemented.

## When/where questions

Alongside the how questions are the 'When will you ...?', 'Where will you ...?', 'With whom will you ...?' questions. Again, these presuppose that action will be taken. Asking 'Where is the best place to do this?' rather than 'When will you do this by?' uses the concepts of time and space and suggests that the coachee will come up with suggestions.

## Avoid why questions

When the question 'Why?' is asked, the answer that follows often allows the coachee to give lengthy explanations of their present situation and the history behind it which can be detailed and confusing. The whole idea of coaching is to lead the coachee out of the situation they find themselves in. 'Why?' can also imply judgement (as in 'Why did you do that?') so it is best avoided.

# Probing questions

A probing question presupposes that some action has to be taken. For example, 'What will you be doing differently in your school?'

Asking the question 'What else?' invites further information and can be asked again and again to draw out additional information. Sometimes people need time to think about the answers to these penetrating questions, so make sure you adopt a gentle approach.

Asking, 'Who will know that this coaching book has been of use to you?' invites the coachee to look at the question through the eyes of another and presumes that something will indeed be different.

'What else will they be doing?' invites the coachee to reflect and think about what might happen.

## Other types of questions

Every question a coach asks has a specific purpose. They can be classified in many ways but what follows are some suggestions to use at particular moments in your conversation.

| Type of question | Example | Purpose |
|---|---|---|
| Clarifying | What does that mean?<br><br>Could you be more specific?<br><br>How would an objective observer describe this situation? | To find out the facts. To increase understanding. |
| Reflecting | What is another way that you could ...?<br><br>What would have to change in order for X to happen?<br><br>What criteria did you use to ...? | Reverses a statement or question by rephrasing and sending it back to the coachee. Keeps the coachee talking. |

| Type of question | Example | Purpose |
|---|---|---|
| Leading | I think it's a shame that you don't enjoy teaching that class – don't you? | The answer is given in the question. Dangerous if used inadvertently. Good for testing a reaction or relaxing a nervous person initially. |
| Hypothetical | If you had to do a lesson on X tomorrow what strategy would you use? | Good for testing possible reactions to certain situations. |
| Challenging | What is actually preventing you from ...? Why do you think this is the case? What gives you the most anxiety here? What is the truth here? | Unblocks barriers to progress. Greater awareness of the problem giving a different perspective. Coachee may need time to think about their answers. |

| Type of question | Example | Purpose |
|---|---|---|
| Reframing | You said you haven't seen progress with the group, but when have you seen progress? | Invites the coachee to re-examine a belief/evidence. |
| Incisive | What could you do if resources were not an issue? | Temporarily lifts limiting beliefs. Stimulates new ways of thinking and new ideas. |

## Closed questions to conclude

Towards the end of a coaching session, it may be necessary to focus on concluding the discussion. The coach then needs to help the coachee limit their answers by asking them either/or questions or closed questions which aim to get the coachee to agree to take action or get a yes/no response. Examples might include:

▓ Was that strategy useful?

▓ Is that something you would be willing to do?

A timely closed question can provoke or confirm a decision or a conclusion, but asked too soon and it could suggest the coach is impatient.

A coach should take us on a journey to a destination, which is a useful analogy of what coaching is about. They support the coachee in moving forward towards their goal and, for the purposes of this book, the goal will be in line with the consistently improving school. That may be what we mean by coaching with edge!

## Finally

Remember to have an attitude of curiosity when asking questions and to keep an open mind. This suggests that the coach does not have all of the answers and is not an 'expert' but someone who genuinely wants to understand the situation. A good coach, just like a good teacher, will use questions that encourage the coachee to think. There will be times when the coach will need to be comfortable with holding silence to give the coachee space to think about their answers rather than interrupting a chain of thought.

## At a glance

■ Develop open questioning skills that give ownership of change to the coachee.

■ Create rapport with the coachee through body language that mirrors theirs and sincere interest in their answers to questions.

■ Use questions to gain vital information that will help the coachee move towards their goal.

■ Ask questions that suggest choice and promote a feeling of ownership of decisions.

■ Avoid 'why' questions but encourage practical solutions that promote action.

■ Close the session with a confirmation of a decision about the action to be taken.

■ Always be endlessly curious about your coachee and use your questions to make them think more deeply about motivation and outcomes.

## Chapter 6

# A coaching framework

The process of coaching is a relatively simple one. However, without proper planning and preparation it can be disastrous. Team members are often 'coached' with no awareness of what is expected of them in the first place. This can create confusion, frustration and stress.

In order to avoid this happening it is useful to follow a procedure, not just for the coaching session itself but for the entire process. The following describes a method of doing this in a results-driven environment.

## The first meeting: structuring the coaching engagement

This not only means agreeing on where, when and how often meetings take place, it also means being clear about why they are taking place and establishing ground rules for the entire engagement. These are important for the results-driven nature of the coach–coachee relationship to operate effectively.

When establishing exactly what the ground rules are, the coach will be in charge and up-front; setting out the essentials is not a process of negotiation but one of clarification.

Ground rules should cover the following key areas:

- Confidentiality, expectations and commitments.
- Reporting relationships.
- Methods of information gathering.
- The way objectives will be agreed upon and measured.
- How progress will be monitored.
- What sort of evidence of progress will be collected.
- Frequency of contact.
- How, why and when the engagement will come to an end.

Clarity and full agreement here will go a long way towards removing obstacles and barriers to achievement, ensuring speedier and more successful outcomes.

Writing this down as a short coaching agreement is important. It should be used to signify the determination of both parties to make it work. An example of a coaching agreement can be found in Appendix 1.

## Chapter 6

# The iSTRIDE model

There are many models of coaching available, but one that is most useful for schools is the STRIDE model (see Thomas, 2005: ch. 2). What follows is an adapted version of the model – iSTRIDE – which is simple, easy to use and implement, yet offers a rigorous and flexible approach.

It is as well to remember that it is only a model: it is not meant to be prescriptive or rigid but organic in nature. With iSTRIDE, coaches can move backwards and forwards along the coaching continuum, using a blend of techniques as appropriate for the coachee. Flexibility and adaptability are always essential to support and meet the coachee's needs.

iSTRIDE is a structured coaching conversation which normally lasts for about 50 minutes, but can also be very powerful in a 10-minute coaching intervention. It is made up of seven steps as the acronym suggests. These are described below, with examples of useful, non-directive questions for each step supplied later. Can you see where coaching conversations you have had in your own workplace would fit into this model?

| i | **Information gathering** |
|---|---|
| | Determining the coachee's issues, goals, confidence levels and finding relevant evidence |
| S | **Strengths** |
| | Paying attention to the coachee's strengths and maintaining them in a resourceful mindset |
| T | **Target/goal-setting** |
| | Identifying the target to be achieved and exploring the motivation to achieve it |
| R | **Resources/reality** |
| | Exploring the current situation in relation to the target and identifying limiting beliefs |
| I | **Ideas/strategies** |
| | Seeking ideas that might help achieve the desired target and overcoming limiting beliefs |
| D | **Decisions** |
| | Selecting the most appropriate option from the ideas generated and rehearsing success |
| E | **Evaluation** |
| | There are two parts to this phase: evaluating the solution *now* (exploring a commitment to agree decisions) and evaluating *later* (agreeing a time to follow up on the actions taken arising from the decision) |

Adapted with permission from Will Thomas, *Coaching Solutions Resource Book* (London: Network Continuum Education, 2005).

## Chapter 6

## i: Information gathering

In the first step of the coaching session the coach will need to establish with the coachee:

- What the coachee perceives the presenting issue to be.
- The goals they have in mind for their session.
- Their confidence levels.
- What information they may have accumulated from sources the coach does not know about (e.g. past lesson observations, student outcomes, past performance) which may be useful in the coaching session.

When the coach is gathering information is it important that the coachee feels safe and supported rather than confronted, as they may be feeling vulnerable. The coach's role is not to be judgemental but in alignment with the coachee's aims and needs, whilst accommodating the values of the school.

As some of the language of coaching can be quite challenging, the coach will need to make use of 'softening frames' such as:

- I am curious about ...
- I was just wondering ...
- Just to ensure that I have understood what you are saying ...
- Could you tell me a bit more about ...

This gentler, non-directive way of gaining information and wording questions ensures that trust is not broken and so maintains rapport with the coachee.

## S: Strengths

> People have all the resources they need to succeed.
>
> A principle of neuro linguistic programming (NLP)

Discovering the strengths of the coachee is not done once only, rather it is a continual cycle which will weave itself throughout the coaching conversation and help to maintain a resilient frame of mind in the coachee. When the coachee is made aware of their strengths, they are in a better position to see that there may be a way forward to tackle challenges.

Creating and encouraging an ongoing personal reflection of strengths, and applying them to the current context, can also help the coachee make changes and raise their self-esteem. Strengths should be continually returned to at points throughout a conversation to build and restore a resilient frame of mind.

Links between strengths and individual performance can:

■ Provide an opportunity for the coachee to talk about what is working in their lives.

■ Assist in creating a positive image of the future.

- Clarify and give focus to the positive target the coachee is moving towards.
- Generate a sense of resilience and well-being.
- Above all the coach needs to be *authentic* by being present and listening at a deep level. This is very affirming for the coachee. The coach needs to believe in their coachee – and vice versa.

Enquiries such as 'What has been working well since the last time we met?' or 'What is the most interesting thing that has happened since we last met?' will open the coaching session. Celebrate any successes. Other questions used in this step could include:

- What have you tried recently that worked?
- What has made you feel successful this week?
- What has been your best achievement of the year?
- What went well this week?
- Tell me about your most sparkling moment as a teacher?
- How does your most motivated class respond to you?
- What are you most proud of as a teacher?
- When do you perform at your best?

## T: Target

'Begin with the end in mind.'

Stephen R. Covey,
*The Seven Habits of Highly Effective People*

Identifying an end goal is essential to recognising when the target destination has been achieved. It is at this point that the coaching journey becomes measureable and can be documented to provide clear evidence of progress. If an end target is where you want to get to, then performance targets are the milestones along the way.

Both the performance targets and end targets need to be documented at the beginning of the process. The coach and the coachee will then have a reference point to use when assessing if progress is being made. This will also be helpful if adjustments need to be made during the process.

Non-directive goals are focused on smaller targets set by the coachee. However, as has been discussed above, there may be times when the goal needs to be more directive (for example, if a staff member is required to improve particular elements of their practice).

It is important to understand the impact of language on the target goal. It needs to be framed using positive language with statements which clearly identify what the coachee wants, rather than what they do not want. Statements that begin, 'I wish … ', 'I should … ', 'I ought … ', 'I must … ' and so on can be very limiting and the coach will need to challenge them in order for the coachee to identify their real aspirations.

For example, if coachee makes the statement, 'I don't want to keep struggling with the behaviour of my classes', this is not a target goal. A coach cannot support a coachee to get to where they do not want to go. To open up the situation, a coach may ask, 'What would you like instead?' This question focuses on the positive solution to the problem.

The criteria for the target need to be tangible, behavioural and observable. Statements like 'I wish I could feel more confident with my classes', when reframed by the coach, become 'Which classes are you more confident with?' and 'What will that allow you to do?' Asking the question 'When you are more confident with your classes, what will that allow you to do?' enables the coachee to see the benefits of achieving their target.

When the target goal is set by the coachee, they take on ownership of it. Through a conversation with their coach, a struggling teacher may decide to work on a strategy which will improve their practice. This goal must belong to the coachee because they must be in control. The clearer and more specific the description of the desired target goal is, the more motivational it becomes.

'Well-formed outcome questions' (a term borrowed from neuro-linguistic programming) will encourage the coachee to look at their target goals in a broader context. For example:

▓ *State the target goal positively*: What do you want specifically?

▓ *Create a sensory representation of that goal*: How will you know when you have it? What will you see, hear, feel, be saying to yourself when you achieve it?

▓ *Begin the process*: What needs to happen to start and keep it going?

▓ *Work with others*: Do you know anyone else who has achieved this? How can they help you?

▓ *Put the target goal into a context*: When, where and with whom do you want it?

▓ *Positive effects of achieving the target goal*: What do you stand to win if you gain this? What do you stand to lose? What is the benefit of staying just where you are?

▓ *Resources*: What physical, emotional or financial resources do you need to support you in achieving this?

▓ *Ecology*: What are the consequences for you and others by having things remain this way? Are those consequences worth it?

▓ *Action*: What is the very first step you need to take in order to support you in hitting your target?

Other questions in this step could include:

▓ What is it you would like to achieve?

- What would need to happen for you to walk away feeling that this has been time well spent?

- What exactly is it that will make you feel successful in this?

- What are you building towards?

- What do you really, really want?

- What don't you want?

- What has to happen for you to feel successful?

- How do you know this goal is worth achieving?

- How will you know when you have achieved it?

- What will you see, hear and feel after having achieved it?

- What will achieving this goal do for you/give you?

- How would other people benefit if you reached your goal?

- What is important to you about achieving this goal?

- How much personal control do you have over your goal?

- What can you do yourself to achieve this goal?

- By when do you want to achieve it?

- How will you measure it?

- What is your heart telling you about this dream/goal?

- What is your dream outcome?

## R: Resources/reality

Having understood and clarified the target goal, the coach will now encourage the coachee to reflect on their current reality.

Both parties need to gather clear, focused information about what is working, as well as any barriers the coachee thinks may prevent them reaching their target goal. This may include looking at attitudes to the current situation, relationships with students or members of staff, processes, determining skills, available tools and so on.

The coach will need to use a curious, enquiring tone of voice and softening frames (see page 115) in gathering this information. This will make the exchange seem less interrogative and maintain the sincerity of the conversation, whilst at the same time placing the coachee at ease.

Reframing the coachee's limiting beliefs is a powerful model that can be used to support them in changing their perception of an event and enabling them to find alternative, solution-focused ways of looking at their current situation. It is not about pretending that everything is perfect; instead it offers more ways for the coachee to consider the issues they want to change. By asking the question 'What else could this mean?', the coach is presuming that there are alternative explanations.

When a situation reminds us of a negative experience from the past, getting a new perspective on it changes its meaning, and therefore our response to it. For example, if a coachee says: 'At a conference I really messed up my presentation – I am useless at public speaking', the coach could respond with:

▓ When have you been successful at public speaking?

▓ What elements of your presentation did go well?

▓ What did you learn from this?

▓ What could you do differently next time?

▓ Who could help with this?

▓ What is one small thing you could do right now in order to ensure that your presentations do go well?

▓ Who could help you with this?

▓ How would doing X help?

This kind of questioning focuses a coachee back on their strengths and helps them get into a more solution-focused frame of mind in order to create ideas. Other questions used in this step could include:

▓ Where are you starting from/what have you learnt so far?

▓ What have you done up to now about this dream/goal?

▓ How effective have your efforts been?

▓ What has stopped you doing more?

▓ What have you learnt from what you've done?

▓ What might you have done differently?

▓ What insights do you have about yourself/life in general that are relevant to this?

■ What will happen if you do nothing?

■ What other choices do you have?

■ What skills do you have that you are not using?

■ What is holding you back?

■ What could stop you achieving your goal?

■ What are you afraid of?

■ What is not achieving your goal costing you?

## I: Ideas/strategies

In this part of the iSTRIDE conversation, the coach draws out options from the coachee by asking what they can do to meet their intended target.

Using questioning such as 'What are the options available to you?' and 'What else?' encourages the coachee to come up with multiple solutions. Others could include:

■ What could you do?

■ What could you do differently from now?

■ What must change for you to achieve your goal?

■ What approaches have you seen used in similar circumstances?

■ Who might be able to help you?

■ Who could you learn from?

■ What would a wise old friend suggest?

■ What would you do if you had ... (more time, less time, power, money, magic wand)?

- What is the simplest solution?
- What is the right thing to do?
- What is the most courageous step to take?
- If the constraints were removed, what would you do?
- What else could you do ... and what else could you do ... and what else could you do ...?
- What options would you like to act on?
- What could you do that would make the biggest difference?

The coach can also offer ideas of their own at this point (permission to do this should be sought first). By the end of this part of the conversation the coachee should have a range of options to choose from. Having choices is often motivating.

## D: Decisions

This stage of the process encourages the coachee to decide the best course of action from the options they created in the ideas step.

The coach then checks the usefulness of the decision and the motivation for it through questioning. Some useful questions include:

- What will happen if you do this?
- What will happen if you don't do this?
- What won't happen if you do this?
- What won't happen if you don't do this?

- What is the first logical step? What are the next steps?
- Precisely when will you do this?
- What will it cost you if you don't take action?
- What will you gain if you do take action?
- What might get in the way?
- Who needs to know about this?
- What support do you need and from whom?
- How will you get that support?

The motivation can be checked using scaling questions such as:

- Where would you rate motivation to take the agreed actions on a scale of 1 to 10 your (where 10 is the most motivated)?
- What prevents you from being at a 10?
- What do you need to do to get your commitment up to at least 8?

This provides another opportunity to explore any blocks still present and iron them out.

## E: Evaluation

The evaluation step takes place following a lesson observation or review. It offers an opportunity for the coach and coachee to reflect and evaluate the process and find out if the iSTRIDE process has been responsible for bringing about the desired outcome.

The coach should be able to explain any differences they have seen, heard and felt but will also need to identify some quantitative data (e.g. Did the coachee get a good/outstanding grade during the last lesson observation?).

There are two elements to this stage of the coaching process:

1. Reviewing today's progress and commitment to action.

2. Agreeing a follow-up date to review progress towards these actions.

This is intended to establish accountability and indicate how the progress fits into the bigger picture. Questions used here could include:

- What did you do that was different?
- On a scale of 1 to 10 (where 10 is trying your hardest), how hard did you try?
- What was the hardest thing?
- What was the impact (qualitative and quantitative)?
- How did it make you feel?
- What has happened since?
- How have you changed?
- What will you do next?

## Coaching exercise

Choose a partner to hold a coaching conversation with, using the iSTRIDE model.

Take it in turns to be the coach and the coachee (10 minutes each way).

Think about the personal qualities of a coach. Remain focused on the non-directive approach and use a range of skills from the coaching continuum.

Feed back to each other after each turn:

- What is the issue?
- What do you want instead?
- What are your possible options?
- What steps can you take?

What went well during this exercise? To be a good coach takes time and practice. If you were to do the exercise again what would you do differently? What would you do more of/ less of?

## At a glance

▪ A coaching framework is important if you are to make coaching work in your school.

▪ Coaches will need training and practice to be successful.

▪ Ground rules for coaching will need to be established.

▪ Use of a simple model will promote consistency.

▪ iSTRIDE is such a model with the following structure: establish strengths, identify targets, review reality, find ideas and options for action, make a decision about next steps and, finally, evaluate the outcome through observation.

## Chapter 7

# Embedding the coaching culture for the long term

> 'Developments with the biggest impact appear to be those that involve changes in practice, which will require new kinds of teacher learning, new models of professional development, and new models of leadership.'
>
> (Wiliam, 2011)

There are many benefits to ensuring that coaching is central to your school development plan. A number of these were discussed in Chapter 3 in relation to pressures from external agencies such as Ofsted and the Department for Education.

This chapter aims to consider how an embedded coaching culture can become self-sustaining and create an enquiring, self-improving and happy school for the whole community.

# Coaching as personalised teacher improvement

How do we create a culture where it is normal for teachers to ask for help and to make positive, supportive, professional relationships? A culture where all teachers continually strive to improve their practice through becoming self-critical? A culture where teachers are brave enough to be innovative and secure enough to know that if things start to go wrong, this will not be seen as failure, only as a source of feedback?

The answer is to establish coaching as a culture – as the way for every member of staff to create ownership of their own individual improvement journey. Coaching can offer a personalised approach to whole school improvement and help every teacher move forward.

Coaching can be as simple as a one-to-one structured iSTRIDE conversation (see Chapter 6) following a thought-provoking INSET session. This, in turn, could spark a direct commitment to action and then monitoring and evaluation of its impact in the classroom. By assigning a coach appropriate to the teacher's stage of development, schools can ensure that each teacher gets the correct level of challenge and support. There will also be a record of the action agreed in the teacher's professional portfolio and, later on, an evaluation of the outcomes.

Coaching is a powerful tool which can encourage improvement in classroom practice and which could, if teachers wished, provide a great evidence base to use effectively in their performance management.

# Planning CPD for impact

Coaching is just one aspect of managing the continuous improvement of teachers. This section looks at where coaching sits in relation to other aspects of school and staff development.

With a sharp focus on school performance in the Ofsted framework, it is clear that the staff training in your school needs to be tied to your school improvement plan, self-evaluation process and the outcomes of performance management for individual teachers.

The figure below shows how performance management can be linked to whole school priorities in the school development plan (SDP).

SDP: School Development Plan; CPD: Continuous Professional Development.

These priorities are then put at the heart of the staff CPD programme. The protocols for this process are known and owned by all staff, so that it is very clear what could trigger, for example, capability procedures or additional support. Opportunities for outstanding teachers to lead training and become coaches also provides opportunities for them to further improve. Every teacher – even the best – should be on a journey of continuous reflection and improvement, underpinned by research, training and coaching for all.

A range of lesson observation strategies – from formal graded observations to learning walks and non-judgemental coaching/learning observations – can be used to help ensure that the senior leadership team (SLT) accurately judge the 'typical' quality of teaching provision. It is important to remember that the purpose of lesson observations is not simply to make judgements but to give feedback to help individual teachers improve performance and inform the SLT about what needs to be included in the CPD programme. For example, questioning skills, missed literacy opportunities or pupil response to feedback could be identified as common problems across the school.

Good and outstanding teachers could be encouraged to initiate action research projects, trying out new techniques in their lessons, or be helped to conduct small-scale research on other aspects of classroom practice. The teachers involved could then, either individually or in small teams, present their findings to staff on a regular basis so that professional sharing becomes part of the school culture. This sharing could occur in a seven-minute spot at a TeachMeet, leading a staff INSET group or in a learning forum. Research outcomes can be a simple feedback comment from pupils or quantitative data or video evidence of work in practice. They could be published on a Learning Wall in the staffroom, in a regular teacher's learning handbook or in the school learning blog. (See examples at www.jackiebeere.com)

This process helps every teacher develop through sharing ideas and helps the school community become fascinated and obsessed by opportunities to improve teaching and learning for the pupils. Once this professional sharing is established as part of school culture, coaching will become the way we help each other to acquire new skills and implement new techniques – all in a spirit of lifelong learning.

The outcomes of the research outlined above can be used to inform the school improvement plan and identify CPD that will further help the school improve. For example, if performance outcomes, research projects and lesson observations have demonstrated that assessment for learning is not fully embedded, an inspiring presenter can be booked. Afterwards, the ideas presented can be taken back to departments or phase groups to be discussed and implemented. All teachers could then have a follow-up coaching session to help them plan their own action following the training. If, during the next observation round, some teachers have not improved their practice, they can be booked in for a live coaching observation.

In this an observer watches the lesson but gives feedback directly to the teachers during the lesson. The observer acts as an extra pair of eyes and ears to see exactly how individual children are responding to the teaching and advises the teacher accordingly. For example saying 'Could you explain that again in a slightly different way?' or 'See if John needs some extension work, he's completed it quickly' or 'Gemma is taking a very long time drawing that box'. The teacher is still very much in charge but the observer is helping to show how he/she can be more sensitive to the needs of the class and meet them.

Outstanding lessons are often led by responsive teachers who are flexible and adaptable. This type of in class coaching can really help those teachers who habitually stick to the plan – however well it is working. A supportive word of advice such as 'Try some pair discussion challenges now' or 'How about letting Josh teach the class because he is way ahead of the others' may give some teachers the confidence to try new strategies and take more risks – and thereby become more responsive and flexible. Many schools use electronic ear pieces so that coachees can get advice from their coach watching the lesson. This is an excellent method of giving instant feedback to help improve classroom practice. (See Chapter 4 for more examples of coaching observations.)

## Performance management

Schools have to demonstrate that they are managing the performance of staff in the school and that they are able to accurately evaluate the quality of their provision. They have to gather evidence of observations and outcomes to show any inspection team and answer that crucial question 'How do you know?' Schools also need to ensure that all staff know the timescales and protocols used by the school for perform-ance management purposes so that there are no surprises:

- Capability procedures – staff should know what could instigate capability procedures. For example, 3 consecutive unsatisfactory observations.

- Satisfactory to good – staff should be aware of the expectation that they should be moving toward consistently good teaching. A clear plan of action with a timescale that involves coaching will be part of the performance management process.

■ Good to outstanding – opportunities to plan for improvement towards 'outstanding' need to be available to teachers.

■ Outstanding teachers need to have opportunities to continue learning through coaching others and leading learning.

If every teacher has their own portfolio of evidence from lesson observations, exam outcomes, research projects, pupil feedback, training events and coaching sessions, then performance management is owned more by that teacher who will, in turn, be better able to critically self-evaluate their own performance. Each teacher can then have an individually tailored programme of professional development involving coaching and other training opportunities to help them continually grow.

## Evidence gathering – owned by staff

■ Profile performance using data and outcomes.

■ Grades and feedback from lesson observation.

■ Feedback from pupils.

■ Training and professional development.

■ Coaching contracts and feedback.

## CPD/INSET – linked to self-evaluation

- Mixture of internal delivery resulting from action research.
- External delivery linked to school needs (e.g. literacy, ICT, Ofsted).
- Bespoke and differentiated for various staff groups linked to performance management outcomes.

## Action research projects

These projects are small, simple pieces of research that look at good practice so that it can be shared within the school. It could be one side of A4, a school blog post or a sticky note on a learning wall in the staffroom! Investigations could cover areas such as questioning, plenaries, literacy, independent learning, ICT, learning to learn, assessment as learning and Year 8 able girls/Year 7 free school meals boys/Year 11 C/D borderline/other gap groups and so on.

Follow up *every* externally run training event or INSET visit with action research to evaluate what the impact has been. These can lead to sharing sessions for the whole staff. Schools are running very successful TeachMeets where teachers share two or seven minutes about something that has worked well for them in the classroom.

## Train your teaching assistants to be expert coaches

The importance of the idea that we are all coaches for each other means that instead of telling one another what the answer is, we are helping others to think their way through to new solutions. This is an essential aspect of the work of teaching assistants. Ofsted will be taking a very close look at how teaching assistants support those learners who are most in need of making outstanding progress.

Unfortunately, research by London University's Institute of Education, quoted in the *Times Educational Supplement*, has shown that sometimes the way teaching assistants tell rather than show children, or even do the work for them, actually restricts progress rather than supports it (TES, 2009). If teaching assistants are taught coaching skills they will see how coaching questions help develop the cognitive abilities of their pupils. They will also see how the coaching culture of giving ownership of thinking and decision-making to the pupils will help empower pupils to use a variety of learning strategies and think for themselves.

## Leadership of learning – what do you need to do?

Leading teaching and learning is a key role in school. It often involves managing teacher performance and planning train-ing, as they are so closely linked. Another crucial aspect of this role is leading the coaching programme and monitoring its effectiveness. In summary, the key elements to embedding a culture of continuous improvement may be as follows:

- Performance management is linked to the Teachers' Standards and coaching is used to support staff in meeting the standards.

- A programme of twilight bespoke training sessions built around the school's self-evaluation and lesson observations by the SLT. Teachers can opt in or be asked to attend according to need.

- A team of regularly trained and supported teacher coaches who engage in confidential professional dialogues with their colleagues.

- A programme of formal and informal observations that evaluate the quality of teaching at the school.

- A regularly updated spreadsheet or record of evidence from lesson observations on the quality of teaching at the school. (See www.jackiebeere.com for an example).

- A regular opportunity for teachers to find out from learners about their performance (e.g. focus group interviews/questionnaires or pupil observations of lessons).

- A professional portfolio for all teachers to keep records of their own development, data, feedback, coaching contracts and evidence of their professional development related to the Teachers' Standards.

- An action research group of teachers and students who constantly conduct research into various aspects of school improvement and share this with the staff and leadership team so that all aspects of CPD outcomes are evaluated. CPD is planned rigorously alongside self-evaluation, performance management and the school improvement plan.

■ Middle leaders or Heads of Faculty are trained as coaches and are coached themselves.

■ Lesson observations are used as learning experiences and include formal, graded observations, learning walks and coaching observations.

■ Teaching assistants need to be part of the coaching programme and should be trained how to use coaching questions to promote good learning for pupils.

## Pupil feedback as coaching

When schools use coaching for their teachers, the added benefit can be seen in the way teachers develop a coaching style in the classroom. 'Feedback is the breakfast of champions' may seem a trite cliché, but John Hattie identifies the effective teacher as one who can maximise the power of feedback and has the ability to 'get out of the way when learning is progressing' and give ownership of the learning to the pupil (Hattie, 2011: 16). This feedback is the skill of coaching the child forward in their learning without giving them the answers, but asking the right questions and coaxing the cognitive development that will help them learn to ask themselves those questions in future.

Teachers want to help their learners be the best they can be. Effective written or oral feedback provided in a coaching context as part of a school-wide assessment for learning regime can work well. Ask pupils questions which move thinking forward such as:

- What progress have you made so far towards the learning outcome?
- How do you know?
- What do you need to do next?
- What have you tried before that works?
- How did you arrive at that conclusion?
- What tells you it is right?
- What would motivate you to work harder?

Linking these questions to statements about the pupils' own learning strategies makes them reflect on and become aware of their own processes of learning (they become metacognitive):

- What I noticed was that you didn't write it down straight away but spent time thinking it through first.
- I see that you have included your working on that problem. Does that help with remembering the method?

## Pupils as coaches

Coaching is contagious! As teachers use coaching questions more frequently, pupils also learn the benefits of using a coaching question to help their peers make progress. When pupils are paired up to support each other and peer assess they can use the coaching questions, like those found in chapter 5, and others such as 'How can you improve this story?', 'What other endings did you think of?' and 'If you wrote it again, what would you change?'

We've all been concerned about pupils who hate being judged by their peers, so setting peer assessment in a coaching context will mean teaching the students first about unconditional support for each other's progress and learning. We can also teach them that when they coach one another they are learning about the process of learning (metacognition) and about strategies for overcoming difficulties by seeing how others deal with similar problems.

Developing this coaching role in pupils could include giving particular pupils roles in the classroom where they can develop their coaching expertise. For example, they could become Spelling Ambassadors, Art Advisers or Times Tables Specialists. When extra help is needed by other pupils, the expert can coach them individually or in groups. Try having a Chief Greeter in your classroom to welcome any visitor to the classroom and explain the learning objectives, the activities going on and the progress made so far. This way you have a fast-track way to impress inspectors with the pupils' engagement and inform them of what has happened in the lesson thus far. By rotating this and other roles, the 'language of learning' begins to be used by more and more students. Research shows that the more children talk about the process of learning – even for a short part of the lesson – the more progress they will make. (See Wall et al, 2009.)

# Top tips for a coaching classroom

- Develop teacher and teaching assistant questioning skills around coaching principles.

- Train pupils in coaching skills including listening, developing rapport and questioning.

- Build peer coaching time into your lesson.

- Use coaching questions for peer assessment activities.

- Get the pupils involved in designing their own success criteria and active learning.

- Create an atmosphere in which every mistake is seen as a learning experience.

- Encourage teachers to get constant feedback from their pupils about their teaching methods.

- Encourage pupils to get constant feedback from their peers to help them evaluate their work.

# At a glance school leaders checklist

■ Select inspired and motivated teachers to lead the coaching in your school.

■ Make it clear to all how coaching fits into your performance management and school development strategy.

■ Make sure you allocate time for coaching to enable it to happen effectively (a successful coaching session can take just ten minutes but this can still result in a commitment to action).

■ Senior leaders need to volunteer to be coached as well as teaching staff – this sends out a powerful message about how much you value the process.

■ Ensure all staff have a coaching agreement/record sheet (see Appendix 1).

■ Invite governors to take part in the process and train them in coaching if relevant.

■ Model what you are introducing – share successes and failures.

■ Evaluate your coaching processes and practice to measure impact and develop expertise.

# Appendices

# Appendix 1: Coaching agreement

**Discussion between** .................................................................
**and** .................................................................................
**Time:** ...................... **Location:** ................................................
**Date:** ........................................ **Session** ............ **of** ...............

---

**Focus over** ............................................................... **sessions**

- ▦ Assessment for learning, particularly areas such as peer assessment, self-assessment, the use of criteria for assessment, feedback, assessment through observation, oral assessment, assessment of group work, etc.

- ▦ Teacher repertoire such as questioning, explaining, modelling and managing plenaries.

- ▦ The effective use of starters/lesson reviews.

- ▦ Challenge, engagement and motivation, which might include the use of visual, auditory and kinaesthetic (VAK) techniques.

- Literacy – reading, speaking and listening, and especially extended writing (which is an issue in most subjects).
- Numeracy – key areas are data collection, data handling and interpretation.
- Teaching thinking skills.
- Managing group and collaborative talk.
- Group techniques.
- The use of Philosophy for Children and Community of Enquiry.
- Mind-mapping.
- Differentiation – teaching mixed ability classes or SEN, EAL and G&T students.

**Other** ...........................................................................................

_____

**Details of classroom work:** ...................................................

**Teaching group:** ...................................................................

_____

**Agreed actions/questions to consider:** ...............................

...........................................................................................

...........................................................................................

**Next meeting: Date** ............................ **Time** ..............................

# Appendix 2:
# Coaching evaluation tools

Name .................................................................................

ID# ...................................................................................

Department .....................................................................

Coach ...............................................................................

Session .................................... Date .........................

Looking back over the past five sessions, including today, please help the coach understand how you have been doing in the following areas, where marks to the left represent low levels and marks to the right indicate high levels.

**Individually (personal well-being):**

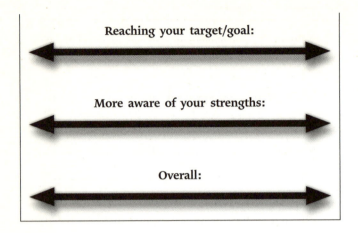

Name ................................................................

ID# ..................................................................

Department ...................................................

Coach ..............................................................

Session ................................... Date .........................

Please rate today's coaching session by placing a mark on the line nearest to the description that best fits your experience.

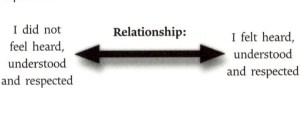

I did not feel heard, understood and respected | **Relationship:** | I felt heard, understood and respected

We did not work on or talk about what I wanted to work on and talk about | **Goals and current issue:** | We worked on and talked about what I wanted to work on and talk about

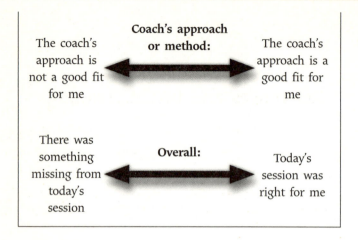

# References and further reading

Beere, J. (2011). *The Perfect Ofsted Inspection*. Carmarthen: Crown House Publishing.

Beere, J. and Boyle, H. (2009). *The Competency Curriculum Toolkit*. Carmarthen: Crown House Publishing.

BlessingWhite (2009). *The Coaching Conundrum Report 2009: Building a Coaching Culture that Drives Organizational Success*. Available at: http://www.blessingwhite.com/cc_report.asp (accessed 7 January 2013).

Buckingham, M. and Coffman, C. (2005). *First, Break All the Rules: What the World's Greatest Managers Do Differently*. London: Pocket Books.

Clutterbuck, D. and Megginson, D. (2005). *Techniques for Coaching and Mentoring*. London: Elsevier.

Covey, S. R. (2004). *The Seven Habits of Highly Effective People*. London: Simon & Schuster.

Creasy, J. and Paterson, F. (2005). *Leading Coaching in Schools*. Nottingham: National College for School Leadership.

Available at: http://thebeechconsultancy.co.uk/uploads/files/leading-coaching-in-schools.pdf (accessed 7 January 2013).

Csikszentmihalyi, M. (1992). *Flow: The Psychology of Happiness*. New York: Harper and Row.

Department for Education (DfE) (2012). *Teachers' Standards*. London: DfE. Available at: https://www.education.gov.uk/publications/eOrderingDownload/teachers%20standards.pdf (accessed 7 January 2013).

Department for Education and Skills (DfES) (2003). *Key Stage 3 National Strategy. Sustaining Improvement: A Suite of Modules on Coaching, Running Networks and Building Capacity*. Ref: DfES 0565-2003-G. Available at: http://dera.ioe.ac.uk/8848/1/DfES 0565-2003G.pdf (accessed 7 January 2013).

Downes, D. and Rock, P. (2003). *Understanding Deviance*. Oxford: Oxford University Press.

Downey, M. (2003). *Effective Coaching: Lessons from the Coach's Coach* (3rd rev. edn). Oakland, CA: Texere Publishing.

Dweck, C. (2006). *Mindset: The New Psychology of Success*. New York: Random House.

Fullan, M. (2001). *Leading in a Culture of Change*. San Francisco, CA: Jossey-Bass.

Hattie, J. (2011). *Visible Learning for Teachers: Maximizing Impact on Learning*. London and New York: Routledge.

Higgins, S., Kokotsaki, D. and Coe, R. (2011). *Toolkit of Strategies to Improve Learning: Summary for Schools Spending the Pupil Premium*. London: Sutton Trust. Available at: http://www.suttontrust.com/research/toolkit-of-strategies-to-improve-learning/ (accessed 7 January 2013).

Hill, P. (2004). *Concepts of Coaching: A Guide for Managers*. Oxford: Chandos Publishing.

Ofsted (2008). *Assessment for Learning: The Impact of National Strategy Support* (24 October) Ref: 070244. Available at: http://www.ofsted.gov.uk/resources/assessment-for-learning-impact-of-national-strategy-support (accessed 7 January 2013).

Ofsted (2012). *School Inspection Handbook* (20 December). Ref: 120101. Available at: http://www.ofsted.gov.uk/resources/school-inspection-handbook (accessed 7 January 2013).

Parsloe, E. (1999). *The Manager as Coach and Mentor*. London: Chartered Institute of Personnel and Development.

Reed, J. and Stoltz, P. G. (2011). *Put Your Mindset to Work: The One Asset You Really Need to Win and Keep the Job You Love*. London: Portfolio/Penguin.

Starr, J. (2008a). *Brilliant Coaching: How to be a Brilliant Coach in your Workspace*. Harlow: Pearson Education.

Starr, J. (2008b). *The Coaching Manual: The Definitive Guide to the Process, Principles and Skills of Personal Coaching*. London: Pearson Prentice-Hall.

Taylor, D. (2002). *The Naked Leader*. Oxford: Capstone Publishing.

TES (2009). TA support makes pupils worse off in core subjects. Available at http://www.tes.co.uk/article. aspx?storycode=6022221 (accessed 21 January 2013)

Thomas, W. (2005). *Coaching Solutions Resource Book*. London: Network Continuum Education.

Thomas, W. and Smith, A. (2004). *Coaching Solutions*. Stafford: Network Education Press.

Thomas, W. and Smith, A. (2009). *Coaching Solutions: Practical Ways to Improve Performance in Education*. (2nd Edn) Stafford: Continuum.

Tolhurst, J. (2006). *Coaching for Schools: A Practical Guide to Using Coaching to Build Sustainable Learning and Leadership in Schools*. Harlow: Pearson Education.

Vass, A. (2008). *Coaching and Mentoring for Leaders*. Tonbridge: Monro Training Services.

Wall, K., Hall, E., Higgins, S., Leat, D., Thomas, U., Tiplady, L., Towler, C. and Woolner, P. (2009). *Learning to Learn in Schools: Phase 4. Year 1 Report*. London: Campaign for Learning. Available at: http://www.campaign-for-learning. org.uk/cfl/assets/documents/OtherDocuments/Learning%20 to%20Learn%20Phase%204%20-%20Year%20One%20 Report%20FINAL%281%29.pdf (accessed 7 January 2013)

Whitmore, J. (2009). *Coaching for Performance: GROWing Human Potential and Purpose – The Principles and Practice of Coaching and Leadership* (4th edn). London: Nicholas Brealey Publishing.

Wiliam, D. and Black, P. (1998). *Inside the Black Box: Raising Standards through Classroom Assessment*. London: GL Assessment.

Wiliam, D. (2011) *How do we prepare students for a world we cannot image?* Available at http://dylanwiliam.org/Dylan_Wiliams_website/Presentations.html (accessed 23 January 2013).

978-178135102-4

978-178135100-0

978-178135090-4